GET HAPPY

MAKE YOUR DREAMS
COME TRUE NOW!

GET HAPPY
Make Your Dreams Come True Now!
By Marc Griffiths

ISBN: 978-0-9989674-3-1

Cover Design & Internal Layout: Jonathan McGraw

All correspondence to: info@getoutyourbox.com

DISCLAIMER

Following the advice in this book could make you millions of dollars and completely transform your life. On the other hand, it may not, and you could hurt yourself in the process. So, regardless of the claim I just made, and the claims I made on the front cover, back cover, and throughout this book, I make no claims whatsoever. Use at your own risk. Don't blame me or the publisher for anything bad that happens to you while trying to implement advice in this book.

However, if things *should* work out well for you, and you make millions and transform your life, please let me know so I can say, "I told you so!"

Also, if there is any reason you don't feel this book deserves a 5-star review on social media, please let me know. If you feel it does deserve 5-stars then let everyone else know!

That was funny...even if he did say so himself!

DEDICATION

With thanks to my loving wife and entertaining children, without whose help I would have finished this book in half the time!

...and thanks to me.

...and me.

CONTENTS

FOREWORD

Dear Reader,

I have been asked to write the foreword.

"Good luck!"

Major Chuckles

Major Chuckles

INTRODUCTION

THE ONE EASY STEP TO BEING A WINNER!

Once upon a time you were a sperm. You shot into your mother's fallopian tube with thousands of other sperm. Pushing and shoving, you fought your way past desperate competitors. You saw the egg! Would you win? You did! You got there first. You won!

You started life a winner. You still are one.

THE ONE EASY STEP TO BEING A WINNER IS TO REALIZE YOU ALREADY ARE!

But then life kicked in. Things didn't turn out the way you thought they would. You had to deal with hardships and disappointments, and suddenly, at this moment, you find this book in your hand, which is a book about how to make your dreams come true. Is it any good? Is it funny? Will it really help you? Can your dreams really come true? I believe they can. I believe this book has found its way into your hand at just this moment for a specific reason and that your dreams really *can* come true.

It doesn't matter what's happened before. You may have won a few and failed a lot. Maybe you've been thrown curveballs that weren't your fault. As you pick up this book I want to tell you that today is

I have decided that this will be a very good year.

16

a new start. It's still "Plan A" for your life. It's time to begin again. Let's keep the good and throw out the bad. Your history doesn't define you, your future does. Life's too short to waste. It's time to start living.

Everything in your life is about to change. If you don't like something then we're going to change it. The only exception to that is your relationship. If you don't like your relationship, then first we change you. After that, we are allowed to change the relationship.

So what's this book about? What are you going to learn? What will you walk away with?

I hate unfulfilled potential. I hate seeing unhappy people living unhappy lives. I want you to be happy and successful, and a huge part of that is seeing your dreams come true. We're going to talk about dreams and what they are. I'm going to fill you up with motivation and give you the secrets that will open the doors you want. I'm going to shift your mindset so the lights come on.

This isn't a book about checking a bucket list or teaching you how to accomplish a set of goals, although those are important, and I will address them. This book is about extracting every bit of potential inside you. It's a book that digs deep to excavate real desires. It will teach you to soar on clouds, rediscover forgotten dreams, and it will arm you with weaponry to plunder all castles of impossibility.

Your creativity is about to be kick-started and your imagination ignited. Your fuse is about to be lit, and by the time you've finished this book you will be on fire, pumped up, and equipped to achieve your dreams. You are about to start living life the way it should be lived, fulfilling every bit of purpose you were born for.

What is your dream? Is it to have the beach house, the luxurious car, and the promotion? Or maybe it's to start a charity, make a difference in the world, and have a happy family. Are the people who have these things smarter, more entitled, and luckier than you? No! But they do know and are doing something differently, and I'm going to show you what and how.

You're about to move from being a victim to a winner. You're about to move from hoping things happen *to* you to making them happen *for* you. If you want to live the life of your dreams, then NOW is your time!

In this book there are secrets, ideas, and inspiration. Take the key points, make a note of them, and file them away. Keep them for a time when you need them to unlock a specific door to get you where you want to go.

Today I lock the door to my past and open a new door to my future.

There are also bags full of encouragement and trunks full of motivation. You'll need these too. We all need encouragement, and this book drips it.

18

Hang on, keep turning the pages, and let it pull you into your purpose and towards your dreams.

It sounds like this will be a really good self-help book!

You think so?

Yes, as a perfect door wedge!

"If you want a happy life tie it to a goal, not to people or objects."

ALBERT EINSTEIN

CHAPTER 1

DISCOVER THE BEST LIFE YOU CAN LIVE!

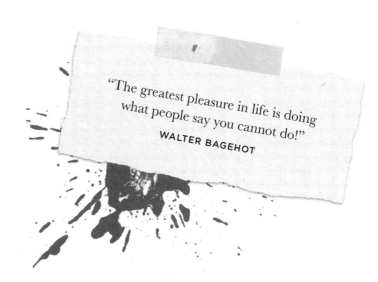

"The greatest pleasure in life is doing what people say you cannot do!"

WALTER BAGEHOT

I began to dream when I heard the story of the man who sold the Brooklyn Bridge. He was sitting in his armchair, just outside New York, watching the dismantling of the old wooden bridge on national news.

While he is watching, he has a creative idea. It's a risk, but he impulsively acts on it. He dials the number of the company doing the demolition. He actually sees the truck driver, standing behind the CNN news reporter, answer his phone live! The man asks the driver, "What are you doing with all that old wood? Would you be willing to drive it over to my place for $500?"

"Easy money," says the truck driver, who proceeds to dump tons of old wood into the man's back yard. The man then begins to cut the wood into small pieces and sell it. "Would you like to buy a piece of the old Brooklyn Bridge?" And people did. First the local and then the national press got hold of the story: "MAN SELLS OLD BRIDGE!" The man went on to make millions of dollars selling slithers of old wood.

What was cool about this man was that he was also an author. He'd written and sold ten books, all best sellers, selling over a million copies each. The same man was a brain surgeon. But what his students didn't know was that, on weekends, he'd commute into New York, star on stage on Broadway and then volunteer in an orphanage on Sunday. He's piloted a plane and a submarine, and as I heard the story, he was canoeing up the Amazon.

I sat there amazed, dumfounded, and blown away by the exploits of this inspiring man. It was a life-changing moment. I'd been taught to go to school, get a job, work hard, and pay off my mortgage. From then on I decided to live a life like that. I wasn't going to live a boring life anymore. I committed, in my heart, to do whatever it took to extract every bit of my potential and live the most amazing life I could possibly live.

You choosing to live a great life is not selfish. It's the best thing you can do because after you have the car, the mansion, and the money, you'll realize those things don't bring you all the happiness you thought they would, and you'll start to reinvest back into the world to find your happiness. In doing so, you'll make it a better place. Being small and playing it safe doesn't help the world. The world needs you to make your dreams come true.

And so the adventure begins.

Everyone's different. Everyone is dealt a different hand when they are born. Someone who is born in poverty in the slums of Manila starts with a different hand than someone who is born into a millionaire paradise in Santa Monica. It's not about the hand you're dealt. It's about playing the hand you have been dealt well! Play it to the best of your ability and finish the game.

My wife was born into poverty and abuse. Her father was tragically killed in a car wreck when she was two, and she was instantly dealt a losing hand. But she hung on. She traded her low cards for higher ones and has now triumphed as a great mother and an inspiration to many young girls.

Thank you for investing in yourself. Thank you for reading a book about YOU. It's the best thing you can do for you. Why? Because, as you're inspired and encouraged, all the positivity will flow into your family, your work, and the world around you. Life from this moment on is a blank canvas. You can create and paint anything. Not everything, but anything. Anything! If you don't like your job, then you can pack it in today. If you want to go to Iceland, you can book a ticket this evening. Anything is possible! Life from now on is officially a blank canvas!

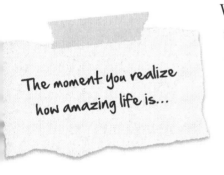

The moment you realize how amazing life is...

We are going to turn your life into a masterpiece. You are going to turn from a chameleon, a creature that is influenced by your circumstances and what others think, into a paintbrush. Your world is going to be exciting, creative, and full of all the color you want!

So, before we start, let's play a game. Here's a list of random dreams and experiences. I want you to look down the list and check off any that you may have done.

How many have you done?

- ☐ Stayed overnight in a monastery in silence
- ☐ Met a celebrity
- ☐ Been on national news
- ☐ Whitewater rafted
- ☐ Piloted a flight simulator
- ☐ Blackwater rafted in New Zealand
- ☐ Swam with sharks
- ☐ Gorilla trekked in Africa
- ☐ Danced at a summer music festival
- ☐ Given a speech on a big stage
- ☐ Been on a TV talent show
- ☐ Touched one of the ancient "Wonders of the World"
- ☐ Driven a tractor
- ☐ Kissed someone under the Eiffel Tower
- ☐ Fired a gun
- ☐ Comforted someone as they died
- ☐ Visited a sick person in the hospital
- ☐ Had a spiritual experience that "blew you away"
- ☐ Driven a speedboat
- ☐ Gone scuba diving off a tropical island
- ☐ Fed an elephant
- ☐ Ridden a camel
- ☐ Galloped on a horse in America
- ☐ Got lost in a maze

- ☐ Babysat someone else's children
- ☐ Held a newborn child
- ☐ Written a book
- ☐ Lived in London
- ☐ Hiked into the Grand Canyon
- ☐ Trekked through Yosemite National Park in the snow
- ☐ Driven over the Golden Gate Bridge in San Francisco
- ☐ Ridden a rollercoaster sitting in the front seat
- ☐ Built your own house
- ☐ Owned chickens
- ☐ Lived on a farm
- ☐ Held a tarantula spider
- ☐ Stopped and listened to a homeless person
- ☐ Milked a cow
- ☐ Bought a stranger their dinner
- ☐ Eaten curry in Asia
- ☐ Been penguin watching in the wild
- ☐ Paid for the stranger in the car behind you in a drive-through
- ☐ Played guitar on stage
- ☐ Dressed up as a clown
- ☐ Caught a pig
- ☐ Walked a dog from an animal shelter
- ☐ Lived in California
- ☐ Walked down a red carpet
- ☐ Petted a koala bear in Australia
- ☐ Worked in an orphanage

- ☐ Run a marathon
- ☐ Stood in Times Square
- ☐ Kayaked with manatees in Florida
- ☐ Read a story to school children
- ☐ Refereed a sports game
- ☐ Worked on a cruise ship
- ☐ Sweated in Death Valley
- ☐ Boxed with gloves
- ☐ Seen a miracle
- ☐ Ridden a scooter through a tropical Island
- ☐ Delivered mail
- ☐ Iced a cake
- ☐ Bargained in Bali
- ☐ Been on a boat in the ocean in a storm
- ☐ Captained a sports team
- ☐ Had dinner in a pitch-black restaurant—where you can see *nothing!*
- ☐ Had a Turkish bath in Budapest
- ☐ Lost over 15 pounds to reach a weight goal
- ☐ Climbed a mountain to watch the sunrise
- ☐ Floated in the Dead Sea
- ☐ Walked the Camino in Spain
- ☐ Been skiing
- ☐ Sat in hot springs in Colorado
- ☐ Hiked in Canada
- ☐ Donated to charity
- ☐ Paid over $500 for a meal

- ☐ Eaten lamb in Greece
- ☐ Drunk wine in Venice
- ☐ Picked up litter that wasn't yours
- ☐ Been in a movie
- ☐ Stared through the bars at Alcatraz
- ☐ Stood in silence in Auschwitz
- ☐ Spoken at a funeral
- ☐ Received a standing ovation
- ☐ Swam with dolphins in New Zealand
- ☐ Started your own business
- ☐ Parasailed
- ☐ Scored a goal at Manchester United

I'm a celebrity! You can check that box!

In your teenage dreams!

How did you do?

I hope you didn't tick them all because that's *my* life! That's a bucket list of dreams that I've actually done and no, I didn't score a goal *for* Manchester United, but I did score a goal *at* Manchester United! Tick!

I've accomplished most of those dreams with hardly any money. Yes, I needed money for flights and for some of the bigger adventures, but I saved and worked and made them happen! I did them. I didn't just talk the talk. I walked the walk, and there are a lot more dreams that I'm working on and still want to achieve. Will I achieve them all? No, but when I get to the end of my life I will be able to say that I lived the type of life I wanted to live. I want to live an exciting and happy life!

How about you? How many did you tick? Maybe only two or three? Good! Because you have different dreams, different talents, and different skills than me. Achieving dreams also makes you an interesting person. You have lots to talk about and more likelihood of having something in common when you meet strangers. I've also failed a lot too. I've had no work, been scared to pay the bills, battled addiction, been torn between the pull of my family and the desire of my dream, been confused over what path to take, and have failed in business. Yet, each one of those was an opportunity to learn something new, to acquire wisdom and confidence, to enable me to climb higher in life.

Who am I? Never let *who* you are become mixed up with *what* you do. I'm *Marc Griffiths*. I'm a son, a dad, and a husband. The

He's been my assistant for years. He's good at listening when I talk! He's a bit cheap though— all my shirts have holes in the back!

29

achievement of my dreams gives me great pleasure and brings me contentment and happiness, but it doesn't determine *who* I am. Never attach your identity to what you do. We live in a world where status is achieved by going to a certain college, owning a fancy car, or living in a big house. This never ending quest for identity can lead to burnout and is the underlying cause of many social problems in society.

Andrew Agassi, after winning a tennis world championship, was quoted as saying, "I am now top of the world, but I feel nothing!" The accomplishment of our dreams and what we do must be kept separate from who we are. Inner peace, identity, and ultimate happiness are an inside job and a subject that I cover in a different book.

So what do I do? I'm an inspirational ventriloquist, an author, and an expert on happiness and living with purpose. That means I have a lot of fun and laugh regularly!

Marc will tell you that I taught him everything he knows, but I taught him much more than that.

My work gives me so much satisfaction because I get to both entertain and inspire my audiences. I've now spoken in over 5,000 venues to more than a million people, giving them life wisdom on how to live awesome lives. I'm going to teach you some of those secrets in this book and give you my expertise so you don't have to go through the same mistakes and failures that I, and many others, have gone through.

I have a team that helps me when I step on stage. I'd like to introduce them to you. They tend to have a mind of their own, so apologies if they add a few of their own comments through the book!

THE SPEAKING TEAM

Through hours of boardroom discussions, the speaking team are always formulating new genius inspiration to stop any event from ever being boring!

KEVIN likes to get out his box! He is known and loved by millions! He is the star of the show—with attitude!

MAJOR CHUCKLES caused harm to many in the war—he was the cook! Now partly deaf, he heads up the social media.

THE TEAM love to get out their box and inspire audiences to do the same. Competition to speak is fierce, and only the right speaker for the right event is ever chosen.

Marc, how did a young fellow like you get started as a ventriloquist?

I found a book in my school library when I was bored.

And then aliens captured him and beamed him up into their spaceship for two years! They taught him to talk without moving his mouth. When they brought him back, Marc felt he owed them one, so he carried on.

Incredible!

Don't listen to everything Kevin says!

I didn't. I'm deaf!

"The biggest adventure you can take is to live the life of your dreams!"
OPRAH WINFREY

CHAPTER 2

HOW TO AVOID THE NUMBER ONE MOST COSTLY MISTAKE!

"A dream is a wish your heart makes!"
WALT DISNEY

People with dreams move forwards. People without dreams move backwards.

Corpus Hernandez, charged with criminal possession of a controlled substance, escaped past police officers inside Brooklyn Central Booking and ran to safety. His quest for freedom was short-lived as he was picked up by cops at his mother's house a few hours later.

Not to be outdone, Hector Calo also fled from the law, dressed only in handcuffs and his underwear. What ingenious hiding place would he choose? He was re-arrested shortly after his escape at his best friend's apartment.

Escaped criminals rarely have dreams or goals. They don't expect to escape, so when that unexpected opportunity comes, they automatically gravitate back to their past, which is how they are easily recaptured.

Senior citizens often retire back to their childhood memories. Many of them collect toys or memorabilia that they had as a child. They spend time reminiscing over childhood photographs.

One thing I do—I forget the past.

People with dreams move forwards. People without dreams move backwards.

A lady committed suicide by jumping off the Biloxi Bay Bridge in Mississippi.

A man, who was walking his dog, saw her fall. The man bravely dove into the water in an attempt to rescue her. However, after a few strokes, he realized the tide was too strong and began to cry out for help himself. Hearing his cries, the woman swam over and pulled him from the raging torrents. The journalist who wrote up the story in the local paper said, "It was new hope that saved that lady's life that day! Suddenly she had something to live for. New purpose pulled her forward into life again."

To dream is to hope.

> Keep the dream alive...hit the snooze button!

Ask a couple how they fell in love, and they go all gooey. Ask them why, and they go quiet. You need a why! "Why" pulls you forwards. You get married because you love your partner, but you crash if you aren't going somewhere together. Sometimes your partner may bug you, but a common cause pulls you forward. In its most basic form it's working together to pay the bills. In its truest form it's being united for a common cause and goal through good and bad. Your "why" pulls you forwards together.

Imagine standing on top of the Eiffel Tower with your spouse on Valentine's Day. It's a magical moment, and you can clearly envisage it. You take a mental snapshot of the moment in your imagination and a new dream is born. It's a moment you want to happen. You can see it in the future. It pulls you forwards.

One of my earliest and worst jobs was working in a factory making metal sheets. I worked at minimum wage, and the noise was deafening. While there I observed an interesting fact that I promised myself I'd never forget. I noticed an average employee made seven metal sheets a day, but if he made eight sheets he was paid an extra $10. That simple goal was enough to motivate the majority of the work force. I watched them sweat and shout at each other to reach their goal. The hope of taking home an extra $10 was what motivated them through their day.

In World War II, during the bombing raids, many children were orphaned. These orphans were taken to refugee camps where they were fed, but the children would not sleep. Nothing seemed to reassure them.

Why couldn't the children sleep?

They were worried about starving the next day.

At last someone came up with the solution. As they went to bed, each child was given a piece of bread. If they woke during the night, they would find the bread in their hands. They were given the reassurance that they would have food in the morning. The bread gave them hope.

THE RATS THAT DID NOT DIE

Professor Curt Richter conducted an experiment with rats. He dropped them into a bucket of water and watched them swim. After a short period of time the rats began to drown before they were rescued. After being allowed a few minutes rest, they were again dropped into the water. This time they swam for an incredible 24 hours before they began to drown. The rats were taught to hope. They learned that if they kept swimming they would be rescued. "After elimination of hopelessness," wrote Richter, "the rats do not die."

A dream puts hope in our future. Now we can see what we are aiming at. Hope pulls us forwards and keeps us swimming in the toughest of times. A dream is also specific. It takes you to a specific destination. Without a dream you are left drifting on the sea of chance.

WHAT'S THE CHANCE OF THAT?

You have a 1 in 175 million chance of winning a Powerball lottery. There is a greater chance of you getting attacked by a shark at 1 in 11 million. The chance of getting a royal flush in poker is 1 in 649,739, and you have a seven times greater chance of dating a supermodel at 1 in 88,000. What's the chance of being "knocked-off" by your pet? In 2005 there were ten cases involving dogs shooting their owners, but only one case involving a cat!

> That was my favorite paragraph!
> I have a chance to date a supermodel!

> I think you have impossible odds!

Don't let chance dictate your life. Let your dreams steer you purposefully to where you want to go.

CHILDREN'S DREAMS

In 2007 I was asked to survey school children in Cheshire, UK. I used my puppets to conduct a fun project, extracting information from children regarding bullying. My qualitative and quantitative research was so unique and informative that it won the LARIA National Research Award. Part of my survey questioned children about their dreams. We found that most young children had dreams. They knew that they wanted to be builders and firefighters when they grew up, but older children had less aspiration. By the time they were ten, their dreams were already slipping away. They had no clue what they wanted from life.

Dreams take you somewhere.

A kick in the pants will take you further!

I can't find my pants. They're camouflage. I've been looking for them all day!

THE "WHY"

What's your dream? Shut your eyes and picture it happening. How are you feeling? That is your why, your driving force. It is the reason that will empower you to overcome every disappointment and circumstance that may try to stop you getting there.

HALF WAY HOUSE

There is a team building retreat center in the Alps where businesses send employees to bond by climbing together. Interestingly, the same routine happens every day. Excited new walkers arrive, pull on their boots, gloves, and backpacks, and ascend up the mountain. Around lunchtime they come to what is known as the "Half Way House." Throwing their backpacks on the floor, they all pile into the lounge to enjoy the piano, beer, and log fire. When lunch is over, and it comes time to put on their boots again, the majority of walkers decide they've had enough and happily choose to keep partying, while the smaller group head into the snow and back up the mountain. At around 4 p.m. the walkers reach the peak and ring the summit bell. The group who chose to stay behind swarm out onto the Half Way House balcony and gaze up at their friends waving down at them from the summit. The party atmosphere instantly changes to one of silence and regret, with everyone having the same overriding thought, "That could have been me!"

I don't know why you're reading this book. Maybe it's a half-way point in your life. The good news is that most goals are scored in the second-half of the game. I'm glad you're holding this book in your hand. It's time to get motivated again. It's time to dream, and to set new goals. You've been stuck at Half Way House too long. Your mountain top is calling.

Those mountains you carry—those are the ones meant for climbing.

Do you see your dream? Your castle in the sky? Do you want to ring the bell one day? To live a life of no regrets? Maybe it's time to resurrect a childhood dream? It's time to put your boots back on and climb again.

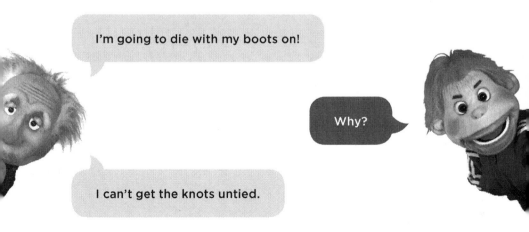

I'm going to die with my boots on!

Why?

I can't get the knots untied.

"All things are possible for those who believe!"

CHAPTER 3

HOW TO AVOID THE NUMBER ONE MOST COSTLY MISTAKE!

"Throw your dreams into space like a kite and you do not know what it will bring back; a new life, a new friend, a new love, a new country."

ANAIS NIN

I went to the local second-hand store to find my wife a present.

Cheapskate!

I found an old oil lamp. Amazingly, when I gave it a clean, a real genie appeared! The genie said she was rather tired after all her work granting wishes, but allowed me one wish. I knew the "genie rules" of course; that I wasn't allowed to wish for anyone to "fall in love with me," and I wasn't allowed to "wish for more wishes!" However, I was allowed one wish. Actually, being a generous guy, I'd like you to have my wish. Here it is. You can have anything you want. *Anything!*

What do you want?

Let me rephrase that. What do you *really* want?

I've asked thousands of people this question. Some just say, "money." I ask them what they would do with their money. After floundering around, they usually decide they'd buy a big house. I say, "Well, that's your dream then! To own a big house!"

What do you want?

Most people don't know. They find the question too difficult. They don't actually know what they really want and so they drift around, being blown by the winds of circumstance, until they wash up in some strange port, wondering how they got there!

Hi Genie! Can I make a wish too?

Yes! You can wish for anything!

Wow! It's my lucky day! I WISH I knew what to say.

That was it. Say goodbye!

Aaaaaaaa!

47

You have the power over the direction of your life when you know what you want. Until then you place the power of direction into circumstances outside of your control.

Let me introduce the *Happy Wheel,* which I talk about in more detail in my book on being happy.

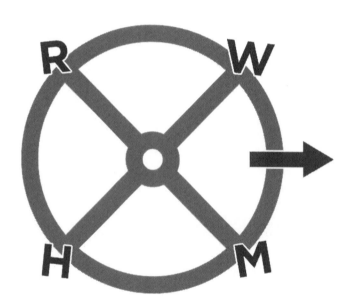

These are five areas of life which we need to be happy in.

We need to be happy at our core. This is the wheel in the middle of the wheel. Unless we are at peace in our inner being, our spiritual being, our soul, at some stage in life our wheel will implode.

We need to happy in the four main areas of life. These are defined by the four spokes on the wheel. We need to be happy in the areas of *money, relationships, health,* and *work.* If one spoke has a crisis or gets damaged then the Happy Wheel struggles to turn efficiently, and we lose happiness. For instance, if you have a relationship breakdown or lose your job, it causes stress and that spoke is damaged. The wheel doesn't turn effectively until the problem is fixed and the spoke mended.

The wheel also needs to be moving forwards. We, as humans, like change. We want something new. Last year's clothes aren't good enough anymore. We want a new experience. We need to satisfy the itch. Unless you are going somewhere and achieving something, you cannot be fully happy. You need purpose. Where are you going?

Primarily this book is about living your purpose. It's about setting goals that move you forwards, but we also need to set goals in each of the other five areas. The overall accomplishment of all these goals brings us great satisfaction and the overall feeling of having lived a successful and happy life.

The achievement of any goal makes us feel successful, but the joy we yearn for is found more on the journey and less at the destination. It's wonderful to have climbed a mountain and the view is spectacular. We feel a great sense of satisfaction at our success. But, if you've ever noticed, there's nothing ever at the top of a mountain. It's momentary. Already you start to think, "What mountain can I climb next?" The joy is therefore found in the climbing of the mountain. If you cannot be content in the climbing, then when will you ever be content? One must then question what the purpose of the climb actually was? Was it striving for meaning or was it to stay busy to cover a deeper issue?

Joy needs to be found on your journey. If a goal isn't going to bring you joy, then why attempt it? If Genie granted your wish and instantly placed you on your mountain top, you'd be happy for a moment, but you'd have missed out on all the sweat, failures, successes, and experiences that would have made it a worthwhile climb. These experiences, like the aggravated rubbing in an oyster shell, are what make the pearl within.

When I was eighteen, I birthed a dream that one day I would be allowed to live and work in America. I travelled to America many times but was never granted a work visa. Twenty-seven years later I sat on a bench, on my own, in Grosvenor Square in London, looking at a freshly stamped work visa in my passport. I ignored the busy hum of traffic as tears welled up in my eyes. No one around me would ever be able to understand my journey to that dream. I was so thankful. It was a wonderful feeling, sitting on my mountain top.

The road to success is dotted with many tempting parking spaces.

WHAT'S WHAT

People get confused between *success, purpose, goals,* and *dreams.* Let me show you the difference.

A DREAM is an idea, a thought. It's imagined. It's dreamed up, but the moment it's put to paper it becomes a GOAL. You now know where you are going. A life list of goals would be referred to as your bucket list. Each goal gives you PURPOSE. Purpose is the *feeling* you have on the journey towards your goal. You can now live a life of purpose because you know where you are going. Eventually you achieve your goal and achieve SUCCESS. Success is the accomplishment of any goal you set yourself.

Therefore, accomplishing any goal makes you a success! This is great news because you can now live a life free of what someone else defines as success. You can make up your own definition of success. You can set and achieve goals that will enable you to get to the end of your life satisfied that you were a success in your own eyes. The definition of success is different for each and every person. Becoming a millionaire is success for one person. Having a 50th wedding anniversary means success to another. Walking to the end of the street without crutches is success to yet another.

• *Definitions of Success* •

"Too many people measure how successful
they are by how much money they make or the
people they associate with. True success should
be measured by how happy you are."

RICHARD BRANSON, BUSINESSMAN, BILLIONAIRE

"Success is waking up in the morning with a smile
on your face, knowing it's going to be a great day.
I was happy and felt like I was successful when I
was poor, living six guys in a three-bedroom
apartment, sleeping on the floor."

MARK CUBAN, BUSINESSMAN, BILLIONAIRE

"I measure success by how many people love me."

WARREN BUFFETT, BUSINESSMAN, BILLIONAIRE

"Success is liking yourself, liking what
you do, and liking how you do it."

MAYA ANGELOU, AUTHOR

• *Definitions of Success* •

"Success is 1% inspiration, 99% perspiration."
THOMAS EDISON, INVENTOR

———————

"Success isn't how much money you have. Success is not
what your position is. Success is how well you do
what you do when nobody else is looking."
JOHN PAUL DEJORIA, ENTREPRENEUR, BILLIONAIRE

———————

"Warren Buffett has always said success is whether the
people close to you are happy and love you. It is also nice
to feel like you made a difference, inventing something
or raising kids or helping people in need."
**BILL GATES, CO-FOUNDER OF MICROSOFT,
WEALTHIEST MAN IN THE WORLD**

———————

And my favorite:

"If you carefully consider what you want to
be said of you in your funeral experience,
you will find *your* definition of success."
STEPHEN COVEY, AUTHOR

What would you like people to say about you at your funeral?

That's one of two great questions I've ever been asked. I spent three days in my imagination visiting my own funeral. What did I want people to say about me? I was then able to work out what success truly meant for me and could set my goals accordingly.

The best question I've ever been asked was after a big stage performance with my puppets, where I'd got a lot of laughs and applause. With sweat pouring down my face, I asked the audience if they had any questions. A small boy raised his hand and asked, "When are we going to have the puppet show?"

What is success to you? Visit your own funeral. Stand on the mountain. What does it look like? What have you achieved? What is it you've done or become?

There are secrets to being successful and I'm going to teach you what these are later in the book, but first we need to define what success is for you. With success comes influence. Imagine an inverted cone shape that flows downwards into your world. That's your *sphere of influence.* Your success is not selfish. It's important, not only to you, but to everyone in your sphere. The average person influences approximately 10,000 people in their lifetime. Being successful helps everyone around you.

PASSION!

People are attracted to people with passion! It doesn't matter if it's fly fishing, rugby, your children, or inter-galactic space travel. When you are passionate, people notice.

If your house is on fire, would you want the firefighters to arrive and slowly start ambling towards your house? No! You want them to leap out the truck with PASSION! Doing things with passion makes all the difference!

Your heart is the core of your being. It contains your passions and desires. That's why a broken heart shatters everything. Love is the greatest human need, which is why our heart is willing to take risks again and again; because it's looking for love, both to give and receive. Knowing what your heart needs helps reveal your passions and desires. When you know these, you are able to set goals accordingly. Your passion will urge you forward because it comes from your core heart desire.

Here are a few great questions to help you work out what your passion is:

1. What can't you stop talking about? If I asked you questions about this subject then you'd happily talk for hours. If you love talking about it then you are clearly passionate about it.

2. What do you love? Is it helping the poor or the homeless? Is it campaigning about the world climate, supporting a sports team, or admiring fine art portraits? If you are willing to sacrifice other areas of your life in return, then you know you love it. Living your passion is always about doing what you love.

3. What do you want to change? Maybe it's injustice, housing orphans, or saving the environment. What makes you angry? What makes you cry and breaks your heart? What can't you tolerate?

Below is a diagram that shows three areas of life.

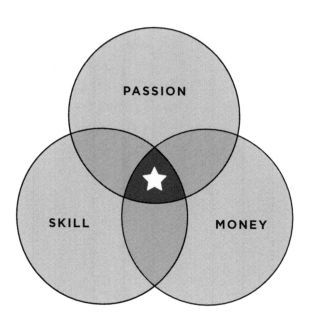

One circle stands for your passion, one for what you are good at, and one for what you get paid for. When these three areas overlap, that is a good indication of what you should be doing and where you should be making a lot of goals.

Many people never see all three circles overlap. They go to work, are good at what they do, but when they return home they go play in their boat, which is their real passion. Life's too short not to live your passion. If your passion is tree frogs, then my advice would be to research, learn, read, talk, and live tree frogs! Join forums, set up *passionfortreefrogs.com*. Very soon you will start to gain a following and you'll be able to start drawing income from your passion. You'll be able to cut back hours on your boring day-to-day job, and eventually you'll start living in the middle of the diagram. Live and breath your passion until you grow webbing between your toes!

YOUR PASSION MAKES A WAY FOR YOU!

Magnus Nilsson's dream was to set up a restaurant. He lived far from the crowds and bustle of city life, but it was his passion! He now lives his dream in Järpen, Sweden. You have to fly, hire a car, and drive through miles of snow-covered sleepy villages to get there. His restaurant has only 12 seats and is now rated as the

19th best restaurant in the world. Magnus's passion made a way for him.

It is no wonder so many people have no idea what their purpose is. They don't know what they want. They've never harnessed their passion or clarified worthy goals, and so they stay busy, trying to fill all their purposelessness inside.

After one of my sessions, a businessman took me to one side. He opened up his battered wallet and showed me a list of dreams he'd set himself three years earlier. They were his treasured possession. His goals gave him purpose.

What do you really want?

Think carefully.

What do you really, *really* want?

I once asked a genie to make my wife 30 years younger than me.

What happened?

The genie made me 30 years older!

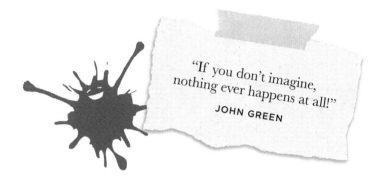

"If you don't imagine, nothing ever happens at all!"

JOHN GREEN

CHAPTER 4

TEN THINGS TO GET SUPER EXCITED ABOUT!

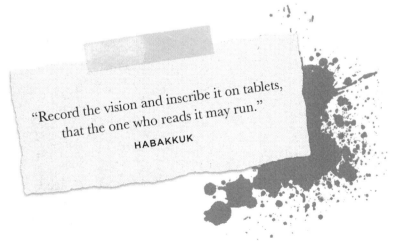

"Record the vision and inscribe it on tablets, that the one who reads it may run."

HABAKKUK

Something amazing happens when you write down your dreams. Harvard University ran a research project on students that had graduated. They found that a unique group, just 3% of Harvard MBA graduates, made ten times as much as the other 97% combined!

What was their secret?

In 1979, interviewers asked new graduates a simple question. "Have you set clear, written goals for your future and made plans to accomplish them?" They found that 84% had no specific goals at all, 13% had goals, but they were not committed to paper, and 3% had clear, written goals and plans to accomplish them.

In 1989, the interviewers again interviewed the graduates of the same class. The 13% of the class who had goals were earning, on average, twice as much as the 84% who had no goals at all. Even more staggering was the 3% who had clear, written goals. They were earning, on average, ten times as much as the other 97% put together!

Something amazing happens when you write down your dreams! Writing your dreams is the first secret to making them come true. You simply move into the top 3% of achievers by writing a clear list of your life goals and dreams.

Did you know that 37.5% of all stats are made up?

After reading this astounding fact, I decided to put it into practice myself.

In 2004 I owned no property. I sat in my rented apartment in Sheffield City Centre in the middle of England. I had a temporary job, making sewage pipes on minimum wage, but I had a

dream that one day I would own my own house. I couldn't afford one. I couldn't afford to buy the most basic of apartments. But I was very specific about my dream as I wrote it down. I was going to own a farmhouse with three bedrooms. It was going to be made of Yorkshire stone, and I even wrote how much it was going to cost me and that it would come with acreage.

Four years later I went to buy and sell some antique furniture, trying to earn some extra cash. I met an investor who gave me advice. He said, "You will never be able to afford a farm. As your earnings go up, so will the housing market, but if ever the chance does come, grab it, as if grabbing the bottom rung of a ladder and then hold on for dear life! Keep holding on and slowly you will be able to climb the ladder and become more comfortable!"

Each Sunday afternoon I would check the property paper. I would drive into the countryside where farmhouses were. "Why are you doing this?" my friend asked me. "You'll never be able to afford one!"

One day a farm came up for sale that was cheaper than the rest. I went to view the property. It was a commercial mess and wasn't for me, but the farmer selling it pointed across the valley to another farm. "Do you see the farm over there? That's coming up for sale soon. Maybe that's for you?"

I thanked him and immediately drove across the valley and knocked on the door. The farmer was disposing of old cardboard boxes to try and make a living. "I've had enough of pig farming," he said. "I want out. If you give me the figure I want, I'll gladly sell my farm to you."

I calculated that if I borrowed all the money I could from banks and family and stretched myself to the maximum, I could just afford what he was asking. It was a huge risk. But I remembered the investor's advice. "If ever the chance comes up, grab it, as if grabbing the bottom rung of a ladder for dear life!" So I did. I bought the farmhouse.

On my first night, I lay looking at the ceiling. It was old, smelly and needed a lot of work. I suddenly sat bolt upright. Four years before I had written my dream down. I had written that I wanted a three-bedroom farmhouse made of Yorkshire stone. I'd even written down how much I was going to pay. My heart thumped. My farmhouse had three bedrooms, was made of Yorkshire stone, and I had paid exactly, to the penny, what I had written down on my dream list four years before! The house was cold. There was no central heating. The previous farmer had cut a hole in the floor so the heat from the log fireplace below could come up into the bedroom, but I didn't care. The farmhouse was mine. I'd written my dream. I'd taken action. I'd persisted and my dream had come true.

Habakkuk says, "Write your dreams and make them clear!"

Harvard University says, "Write your dreams and make them clear!"

My story says, "Write your dreams and make them clear!"

Something amazing happens when you do. It's as if the universe is opened and a supernatural path is created. Sure, you will have obstacles and it won't be easy, but now you know, your subconscious knows and the world around you knows what you want and where you are going, and it moves to help you get there.

"No, I can't write my goals," some people say. "I'm too busy!" Well, if you don't have time to stop and think and write them down, then you certainly don't have time to accomplish them! Like the other 97% of people who don't make their dreams clear, you will be swept along by the currents of life, trying to pay the bills, working to survive, and blaming anyone and anything that things haven't turned out quite the way you expected.

Arnold Schwarzenegger, movie star and politician, says that setting dreams and goals is like piloting a plane. Suddenly you know where to fly. You know where to go. You have a goal.

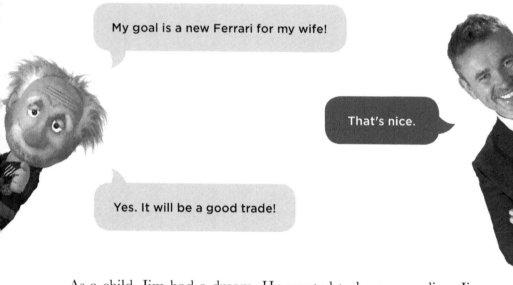

As a child, Jim had a dream. He wanted to be a comedian. Jim used to wear his tap shoes to bed, just in case his parents needed cheering up in the middle of the night. When his father lost his job and the whole family had to live in a camper van, he worked an eight-hour shift straight after school.

Jim debuted as a stand-up comedian at the age of fifteen, and he bombed so badly that it made him doubt whether he could make a living as an entertainer. Fortunately, he persevered and moved to California. In 1985, broke and depressed Jim drove his old beat-up Toyota up into the Hollywood hills. There, sitting overlooking

Los Angeles, he daydreamed of success. To make himself feel better, he wrote himself a check for $10 million for "acting services rendered." He post-dated it and kept it in his wallet.

Nine years later, Jim Carrey was paid a check for $10 million for his movie *Dumb and Dumber*. That year, when his father passed away, Jim Carrey slipped the check in the casket as his gesture of thanks for his father's belief in his dream.

If you want to be successful you need to set out a blueprint of your future. Will it turn out like you think? No, of course not. Things happen. New adventures and new opportunities open up that wouldn't have if you hadn't started dreaming, but at least now you have a map. You know where to sail your ship. The storms may come but you have charted a course and have an idea of where you are going.

You can dream
anything!

Together, we are going to start by dreaming twelve specific dreams.

There are a few rules:

1. **Write them in this book.** Fill in this list. I don't care that you don't normally write in books. Break a habit. Write in this book. Use pencil if you have to. You must write them down.

2. **Dream!** Give yourself time on each one. Stop and imagine. Don't rush this part of the book just to get to the end of the chapter. This section has the power to completely change your life. One dream or one thought changes everything. Stop. Think. Take all the time you need. Nothing around you that you can see has been created without someone first seeing it. You have to see it first, so put on your creative goggles and start to dream.

3. **Be specific.** "I want to look good" is not specific! How do you know when your dream has happened? "I want to be happy!" What does that mean? "I want a happy family?" How can you tell when that happens? You must be specific. The more specific your

dream is the more powerful a goal it is. The more specific your dream is, the harder it is to write down. But the more specific your dream is, the more likely it is to happen. A specific health goal may be, "I weigh 175 pounds." That's a great dream! You are taking ownership. You are writing it in the present tense and you are being specific. You are owning it and imagining it, and you will know when you have achieved it! Be specific!

4. **Dream as if time and money have no relevance.** If you were guaranteed to live another 100 years, what would you want to do? If you had $20 million, what would you do with it? "I'd own a mansion!" Really? "Hmm, on second thoughts I'm not sure I would. I wouldn't want all that responsibility. I'd rather travel." Great! You're getting to your real passion. Dream with no limitations! You can always add limitations later.

5. **Dream big dreams and small dreams.** "I'd like to own a five star hotel property portfolio! I'd also like to wear silly socks one Christmas! I want to snorkel with manatees! I want to own a yellow armchair!" Anything goes. Big and small, your dreams are your dreams.

6. **Create an atmosphere to dream.** Set yourself some time. Go to a busy coffee shop if that activates your brain. Light a candle. Play soft background music. Give yourself time and create an atmosphere to think.

DREAM BIG. DREAM SMALL. DREAM WITH NO LIMITATIONS. DREAM SPECIFIC.

1. **What's that dream place where you want to go?** Remember, be specific! When do you want to go there? Who will you be with? What's the weather like? Imagine being in that place very specifically, and then write down what you picture.

2. **What's your dream occupation?** What did you want to do as a child? Don't be practical. You could still do this. Someone has to. Why can't it be you? What do you want to do?

To play electric guitar!

3. **What's your big dream?** Whatever that means to you. Stop. Think. When you get to the end of your life and think, "Yes, I did my big dream!" What would you like that to be? What's your big dream?

4. **What's your dream adventure?** Where are you? Who are you with? What are you doing? Write down the picture you see.

5. **What's your dream birthday cake look like?** What's it made of? How many layers does it have?

6. **What's a silly dream you have?** You've always wanted
   to do this, but it's a bit silly. Would you like to drive a lawn
   mower? Dress up as a clown for the day? Have a bath in
   chocolate? What's your silly dream?

7. **What's your scary dream?** You want to do this, but you'd
   be a bit scared to do it! Is it to bungee? Swim with sharks? Be
   single? Get married? What's your scary dream?

8. **Who is that dream person you'd like to meet?** Is it a
   movie star? The president? Your future spouse? If you could
   hang out with someone for a day, who would it be?

74

9. **Write down a financial dream.** What do you want to be earning? How much will you save a month? What's your net worth? Write down a financial dream.

10. **Write down a health dream.** What do you want to look like? How much do you weigh? Is it to have plastic surgery? Is it to design a health shake or to be exercising a certain number of times a week. What's your health goal?

11. **What's your charitable dream?** What do you want to do for society? How will you give back? Something for your church? A certain amount of money you'd like to raise at a fundraiser event?

12. **What's your family dream?** Where are you? Who is there? What are you doing?

Congratulations! You just started to dream. You wrote down your first dream list!

Was it easy? Did you find it difficult to be specific?

I did a similar test in a school once. I asked, "Where do you want to go?" A boy replied, "To a Michelin three-star restaurant!" Then I asked, "What job do you want to do?" His answer, "To be a chef!" "What's your big dream?" I continued. "To own a restaurant," was his answer. I have a good idea of what that boy will do when he grows up!

MAKING DREAMING FUN!

I spend time with my 12-year-old daughter. We go out to Starbucks every month with our father-daughter dream book. She draws on one page, and I draw on the other. Every month we pick a different type of dream to draw. We are creating memories. We are bonding together as family. I'm achieving one of my dreams, which is to "date" my children on a regular basis, and because we are talking about her heart desires, I am getting to know her and inspire her to dream.

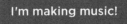

Why don't you do this with your spouse? Start a dream book. Date each other every month for a year. It would draw you closer and inspire you to both move forward towards common goals.

Why write your dreams when you can draw them? Why draw them when you can cut them out? My journal is full of pictures that I've cut from house and travel magazines. Many of them have little ticks next to them. I saw a beautiful picture of a retro chic hotel in Paris. I thought, "Wow! That's amazing! I'd like to go there one day!" I cut it out and stuck it in my journal. A year later I ended up traveling through Paris with my wife. I looked up the hotel and booked us in. It was a beautiful hotel, made doubly enjoyable by the accomplishment of a dream. There is a big tick mark next to the hotel in my journal. Each tick gives me more confidence and drive to achieve the others.

After one of my talks, one head teacher was so inspired that she started her own dream book. It is a beautiful creation, and she has started living life with new energy. She's flown a plane, lost twenty pounds, done a parachute jump, and run several marathons! I think her colleagues feel a little boring when she arrives back at school on Monday morning and starts telling them how she's been on the fastest zip-line in the world, raised hundreds of dollars for charity, and sung in a 100-strong woman choir!

The people in the apartment next door are so rude! They pound on the wall at 2 a.m. every night! It interrupts my electric guitar practice!

Another person told me how they'd created a family dream board. They cut pictures of what they wanted as a family and stuck them on a big board over the kitchen table. The seven-year-old had stuck up a picture of a water bottle. Her dream was to raise $10 for water aid.

Another teacher had turned an old whiskey bottle in his kitchen into a savings jar. As a family they had written down and now practically begun saving towards their dream vacation.

You need dreams in different areas of like. You've just written twelve. You need a dream list of 100 dreams minimum. What did you want to do as a child? What's your passion? If it's to travel then you should have a lot of travel dreams. As you begin to tick them off, you meet people who tell you theirs, which give you new ideas, so you add more exciting dreams to your list.

By dreaming and writing your dreams down, you instantly create new purpose for your life. Purpose is the positive feeling you get as you actively work towards a worthy goal. You've set some goals, and now you have purpose to make them happen!

They never had electric guitars when I was your age.

They never had electricity either!

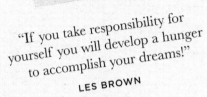

"If you take responsibility for yourself you will develop a hunger to accomplish your dreams!"

LES BROWN

CHAPTER 5

YOU GROW UP THE DAY
YOU DO THIS!

"Leadership is taking responsibility while others are making excuses!"

JOHN C. MAXWELL

"You can destroy the Emperor," rasped Darth Vader to Luke Skywalker. "He has foreseen this. It is your destiny, and together we can rule the galaxy!"

I'm sorry Darth, but Luke had a mind of his own. He took control of his own future. His destiny was not predestined and neither could you twist his arm, the one you didn't chop off anyway! Luke made his own choice. He chose his destiny.

And so do you!

Whether you are taking a step toward your dream today or are doing nothing, you are still choosing a course for life. Your path is chosen, whether it's through a passive or an active choice.

Your life is up to you!

Are you tweeting?

That's just my hearing aid whistling.

Imagine a river of circumstance washing you through life. Passively, you can lay back and let it wash you wherever it flows, or you can make the effort to swim in a different direction. The first one is passive. The second is active. Either way, you are still making a choice. Staying in an abusive relationship, living thirty years in a body you're not proud of, or going to work in a job you hate, are all choices.

Circumstances change. We can't control them, but we always have a choice. We have a choice how we spend our time and money. We have a choice over what we think and what we do. We can choose what to focus on and what to believe. We have choice, which means we have control over our lives.

That's so exciting because if there's anything in your life that you don't like you can change it. You may need a mind shift or a light bulb moment, but you can shift your life into a happier place.

Is it easy to change? No. But it is simple and it is up to you.

Let me introduce two trees. One bears bad fruit. One bears good fruit. When you meet someone who is abusive or rude, it's very easy to take offense. But the reality is that person just displayed their fruit. It wasn't you. OK, so maybe you did pull out a little too fast in your car to

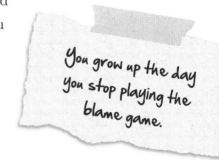

You grow up the day
you stop playing the
blame game.

upset them, but their anger and the way they gestured at you was their choice. They produced some bad fruit.

You can tell what a person is like by the fruit they produce. A joyful person is easy to spot because they are happy and positive. But the fruit we see is never the real issue. Anger and addiction are only fruits of deeper issues. Negative fruit grows from three branches called "justification," "rationalization," and "self-pity." These three branches, in turn, grow from one thick trunk called "blame."

My daughter flew into a huge temper and was banished to her room. She justified her action of twisting her brother's arm. She rationalized that it had been the right thing to do because it was her turn to use the phone, and she certainly felt sorry for herself! Ultimately, she blamed her brother for her misfortune!

Whilst staying in North Wales, I met an American couple at breakfast. I listened as the wife told me how her life was now ruined because of Donald Trump! I said, "It sounds like you've given Donald Trump the power over your life," which had the effect of making her even angrier! She was angry her healthcare was ruined. It wasn't, as she lived in the UK and received free British health care. The reality was she was angry at life and wanted someone to blame. She could have planted an organic garden, educated herself more on her medical needs, taken out health insurance, chosen to exercise or eaten a healthier diet. She had options, but instead she blamed.

Blame is an underlying cause of a huge amount of issues. People are afraid to take risks for fear of being sued. People blame for their misfortune. Suing attorneys pass their costs to the healthcare system that then pass it back to the American public in higher premiums and insurance rates.

We blame our mother and father for what happened to us in childhood. "That's why I act like I do and am who I am! No wonder I am so unfortunate and undisciplined! It's my mother's and father's fault!"

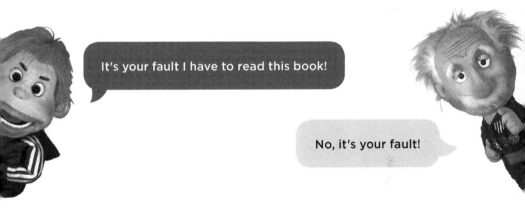

It's your fault I have to read this book!

No, it's your fault!

We justify, rationalize, and feel sorry for ourselves. We keep blaming and running on our busy hamster wheels. Of course we do inherit a way of life and thinking from our parents, but ultimately we have the choice of whether to live a life blaming or one that takes responsibility for our actions. We grow up not when we are sixteen or twenty-one or even when we leave the nest, but the day we pick up the remote control for our lives and say, "From now on, my life is up to me!"

Declare it out loud over your life right now.

Life is just choices.

"From now on, my life is up to me!"

With each choice you build something into your life. Good or bad. You are continually making choices. That's all life is. Choices, like Legos, are building blocks. Decision after decision, choice after choice, create habits, paths, and a whole lifestyle. You choose how you spend every second, and you choose how you spend every dollar. You choose your attitude, where you go, what work you do, what friends you have, and how you spend each evening. If you want your life to move in a different direction, you simply need to make different choices.

It's not about the conditions of your life. It's about your decisions. Change your decisions, and you'll change your conditions. Poor choices lead to a poor life. Good choices lead to a good life. Excellent choices lead to an excellent life.

You don't need more information. You're clever enough already. You already know the answers. That's why I ask you questions. You already know the answers! You're clever. You know what you should be doing and, if you don't, Google will tell you in seconds. Your problem isn't information. You're bombarded with too much information. It's having the wisdom to make the right choices and then the self-discipline to action them.

Be the game changer!

THE LOTTERY LIE

I'd like to give you some money.

$500,000. Here it is:

A lottery ticket. That's real money, right?

A lot of people clearly think so. Instead of making a series of good choices, they carry on their lifestyles, blaming anyone and everything, and buying lottery tickets, hoping it will lift them out of the world they live in. The odds of winning the $540 million Mega Millions jackpot on Friday are roughly 1 in 259 million. Powerball players stand an even worse chance of winning Saturday's $288 million jackpot, where odds are stacked against them at 1 in 293 million.

You have more chance of:

- Being killed by a vending machine at 1 in 112 million.
- Dying from being left-handed and using a right-handed product incorrectly at 1 in 4.4 million.
- Dying in a plane crash at 1 in 1 million.
- Being killed by flesh-eating bacteria at 1 in 1 million.
- Getting struck by lightning at 1 in 1 million.

And people still play the lottery every week! Let's kick the lottery lie out the window once and for all. From now on, your amazing life is up to you!

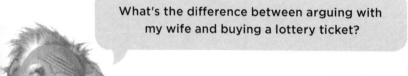

I GIVE YOU PERMISSION!

No one is going to come up to you and give you permission to go for your dreams. People don't care as much as you think they do. When we are young we are paranoid what everyone thinks of us. "What will they think if I wear this or if I did that?" When we get old we wish someone thought of us period!

I am giving you permission right now. I give you permission to go for your dreams, but whether you do or don't is, of course, your choice.

I give myself permission!

To be awesome!

For what?

Good grief! How many Kevins does it take to change a light bulb?

I don't know.

One. He holds it and the world revolves around him!

I am awesome!

EMOTIONS

Don't let your choices be ruled by your emotions.

"But Marc, you don't know how I'm *feeling!*"

Emotions are not there to control you. They're there to guide you into making better choices. The good news is that you can rule over your emotions. If you control your thoughts you can control your emotions. Your mind can only park one thought at a time in thought junction. Why are you continually letting "I can't" and "I'm too scared" thoughts stop at your one and only thought platform?

If you watch horror movies, read tabloids to work, listen to the news in the car, then guess what's going to be filling your mind?

My wife and I have created a family environment that is peaceful and creative. We censor what our children watch. If I want to be happy and inspirational, then I make sure I'm continually filling my mind with happy and inspirational thoughts.

Last year I drove over 40,000 miles on the road. That was often more than six hours of driving a day. I listened to the radio once all year, for about fifteen seconds! Then I went back to my podcasts, CD's, and conversations with friends. I speak to tens of thousands of people in hundreds of venues. I cannot give what I don't have. I need to keep myself happy and encouraged. Be careful what you allow into your mind. You have the power over it, but what you feed it is what will grow and what will start determining your choices.

There are two types of people. Those who say, "I'm going to wait until I feel like it, and then I'll do it!" and those that say, "I'm going to do it, and then I'll feel like it!"

Every thought, every word, and every dollar is a seed. What and where you plant will determine what you will harvest down the road. Make good choices and you'll start feeling good about yourself. Don't let your emotions rule over your choices. If you want to be happier, then make your choices rule over your emotions!

96

TAKE CONTROL

There are no committees on a battlefield. The battle belongs to the commander who takes control and makes calculated, decisive choices. It's not the smartest people who achieve success. It's the people who take ownership of their life, stop procrastinating, and take consistent action towards their goals.

According to a Fidelity study, 86% of millionaires are self-made. Only 14% came from rich families that helped them out. All of them were different. Some were quiet or loud, wildly dressed or conservatively dressed, well-educated or poorly educated, but there were three fundamental qualities found in every one of them:

1. They knew WHERE they were going.
2. They knew WHY they wanted to get there.
3. They took ACTION.

In other words, they all took responsibility for their lives. They stopped blaming. They took their balls out their mother's purse and said, "From now on, my life is up to *me!*"

I walked into a school in Cardiff, Wales. A teacher beckoned me over and whispered how her life had changed since my previous visit. She thanked me for changing her life. Did I? No. She did! I simply gave her hope and inspired her, but she was the one who took action and changed her life.

Your wonderful life is up to you. If you don't take control of it then someone else will and you'll end up living a life serving someone else's vision. So let's take control and do something!

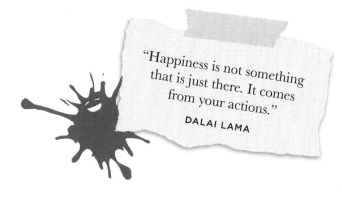

"Happiness is not something that is just there. It comes from your actions."

DALAI LAMA

CHAPTER 6

THE MOST IMPORTANT STEP YOU MUST DO!

"A dream doesn't become reality through magic; it takes sweat, determination, and hard work."

COLIN POWELL

All you need to do is think and believe that you'll achieve your dreams.

NOT TRUE!

Many people think and many people have great intentions, fully believing they will happen.

BUT...

They don't do one thing. They don't take *consistent action every day.* Most people are not willing to commit to moving from what's comfortable into their new, until it becomes comfortable.

One of my all-time heroes is Larry Walters.

LARRY

Larry Walters was a Californian truck driver who, on July 2 1982, decided to do something extraordinary. Larry regularly sat in his backyard drinking beer, wishing that he could have fulfilled his childhood dream of being a pilot. One afternoon he hatched the genius of idea of tying balloons to his garden chair, so he could float peacefully above his neighbors, waving down to them.

Armed with a 6-pack, a radio, and a pellet gun which he would use to shoot a couple of the balloons so he could hover at a comfortable height of around thirty feet, Larry cut the rope. The chair ascended with such force that he dropped the gun and grabbed hold for dear life. He shot straight up with his girlfriend's screams echoing in his ears.

Forty-five minutes later a passenger jet plane swerved to avoid a man floating at 16,000 feet above LA airport! Eventually a couple of balloons popped and Larry descended, striking power cables and causing a blackout in Long Beach. A group of reporters rushed to greet him as he landed. Shoving microphones in his face, they asked him why he'd done it.

"You can't just sit there, can you?" said Larry. "I've had this dream for twenty years. If I hadn't done it, I think I'd have ended up on the funny farm!"

You can't just sit there—can you?

Nothing great has ever been achieved from the comfort of a sofa. Larry is my hero because he *did* something!

This is
what you
will use to
**MAKE
YOUR
DREAMS
COME
TRUE!**

It's very simple. You simply lean the ladder against your dream and climb it. It's that simple and that profound. If you only remember one thing from this book, remember the ladder! You need to place it on a good foundation, lean it on the right wall and climb it, step by step.

CHOOSE WHERE YOU LEAN IT

Be careful which wall you lean it against, because that's where you're going to end up. You don't want to go through life and get to the top of a ladder, only to realize you leaned it against the wrong wall and that wasn't what you wanted after all!

You can choose to climb a little wall or a big wall. What are you going to climb? Will you be happy climbing a little wall? You can play safe or you can risk big. Climb a skyscraper. Climb the Eiffel Tower. Climb a pyramid. Climb big or climb small, but no one will remember you if you climb nothing.

You will never get to your goal if you keep moving your ladder! You need to be decisive. Indecision means the door is still shut. Decision opens the door. If you get sidetracked and keep moving your ladder between dreams then you're not going to get much climbing done. Lots of people have ideas and they climb a few rungs and then get curve-balled by something else, so they stop climbing and decide they want something completely different. They start over again and again, never climbing anything of any significance. Decide where you're going to lean your ladder and keep it there.

You will never get to your goal if you stop for every barking dog.

CHOOSE WHAT YOU STAND IT ON

Your ladder *must* be built on integrity. Integrity is a core value that will break you or make you. You could be the richest, most talented, and most entrepreneurial individual the world has ever known, but if you don't have integrity, your ladder will slip and dump you back on the ground at some point in life. With no integrity it's not *if* you'll fall, it's *when* you'll fall.

What's integrity? Integrity is doing the right thing when no one else is looking. Integrity is honesty. It's adhering to the right values when you can get away with doing the wrong ones. It's being truthful when no one else sees. You know, and you'll always know. With no integrity you can be sailing the high seas on your private yacht with a billion dollars stuffed in your pocket, but you will never be truly happy because you would always have to live with the knowledge that you had no integrity. No one else may know, but you do. It's *impossible* to be fully happy if you don't have integrity.

Integrity leads to inner peace. Inner peace leads to confidence, which underpins all business. If you want to be confident, have integrity. You did the right thing. You're pleased with yourself. Your inner confidence goes up, which leads to increased self-esteem and greater inner happiness.

Integrity leads to faster business. If I want to sell you a car and tell you it has no problems, you'll buy it off me. You trust me. You saved yourself a lot of time and money having it checked. You trusted me, and we did fast and efficient business. Everyone's happier and better off. If I didn't have integrity and knowingly sold you a faulty car, then trust would be broken. My reputation would take a nosedive, and you wouldn't do business with me again.

Integrity and trust go hand-in-hand. Trust is like pushing a bowling ball up a flight of stairs. With hard work you can get the ball to the top. Trust is built a step at a time. However, if I break trust, then the ball falls right back to the bottom, and I have to start again. This is true in relationships. You build trust with your partner. Integrity builds trust, which builds intimacy, which leads to a happy bedroom!

Don't take any moral short cuts. It is *never* worth it and, if for some reason you think it is, then I'll see you back on the ground later in life. Integrity is your solid foundation.

DOES WHAT IT SAYS!

Ronseal made one of the most successful British TV adverts of all time. Ronseal sells paint. One of their ads showed a man painting a fence, drinking from a cup of tea with a dog barking in the background. Nothing happens. The ad tag line is *"Does what it says on the tin!"*

It was such a popular ad because it was straight-up and real. People are fed up of talk. They want action. If you say you're going to show up, then show up. If say you're going to do it, then do it. Talk is cheap. Everyone talks. Not many people act. What you do is what you're remembered for and what you're ultimately known by.

If you eat cheese and chocolate with the occasional piece of fruit, you'll be unhealthy. If you eat broccoli and kale with the occasional cake, you'll be healthy. What you do on a constant basis determines what you become.

People talk a good talk, especially in the States. I can't count the times I've asked people what they do, and they say something like, "I'm a creative artist, a life coach, an author, an entrepreneur, and a business owner!" They then flash their shiny business card, and after another ten minutes of waffle, it becomes clear that they've accomplished nothing and still live with their momma!

People are desperate for identity. They want to look good. They've got the designer shoes and the designer tops and the designer jeans and the designer car and the designer jewelry. Even their underpants are designer! In fact, they're so covered in other people's names, that it makes me wonder if they've forgotten their own name.

I enjoy hiding in coffee shops and being creative. I get a creative buzz being around people and from drinking good coffee. Find your creative spot and use it! One day, in a London back street cafe, the barista started telling me how many guys insisted on leaving her a big tip to show off. "I know they don't have much money," she said, "but they want to be someone so they leave this big tip, trying to fool me that they're rich and they're someone!"

Don't be fooled by the talk and the looks or even the flashy car (that's probably loaded up on credit!). Keep your integrity. Believe in what's right. Put your ladder on a strong foundation.

CHOOSE TO STEP

"Do or do not—there is not try!" Yoda's wise words still echo through the galaxy.

Several years ago I stood nervously, ready to take a penalty kick at Old Trafford, home of Manchester United, the most famous soccer team in the world. The crowd screamed. Would I score? Unfortunately, the crowd was in my imagination. The club had kindly allowed me to make a short movie on the pitch with my puppet! The reality was that I was surrounded by 80,000 empty seats and a small crowd of Japanese tourists! But it was an amazing feeling placing the ball on the penalty spot in the middle of such a fabulous sporting arena.

You must be a *fantastic* magician!

Why do you say that?

You just made 80,000 spectators disappear!

Would I score? I would never know until I actually kicked the ball. I could stare at the goal all day long, but until I moved and kicked the ball I would never score. You have to *do* something if you want to score!

Here are some inspiring true stories of children who did something.

What will you start with?

KATIE

Katie Stagliano planted a seed when she was ten. It grew into a huge cabbage that she donated to feed homeless people. Katie's Krops now has over 100 gardens in thirty-five states and gives thousands of vegetables away. She started with a seed.

WINTER

When her father died of cancer, Winter Vinecki began running marathons at the age on nine. She achieved her dream to be in the *Guinness Book of Records* by becoming the youngest person to run a marathon on all seven continents. Her nonprofit organization, Team Winter, has raised over half a million dollars for cancer charity. She started with a pair of shoes.

CHARLES

As a shy and timid boy, he was often teased and ridiculed. But he was good at one thing—drawing! Charles Schulz went on to create the famous cartoon strip *Peanuts*, which featured the characters *Charlie Brown* and *Snoopy*. He is widely regarded as one of the most influential cartoonists of all time. He started with a pencil.

ALBERT

In 1895 Munich's schoolmaster wrote in Albert Einstein's school report, "He will never amount to anything." He started with his brain.

DAVID

Practicing his soccer skills daily, David Beckham would often play on his own and in the snow. He paid the cost with hard work, and he started with a ball.

VICTORIA

"When I grow up I want to be more famous than *Persil Automatic!*" Victoria Beckham's childhood dream was to be greater than a detergent brand. She achieved it by becoming a world brand, but she started with a dream!

What will you start with?

DON'T LET MONEY STOP YOU

My sister's dream was to be a fashion designer. She started borrowing fashion books from the local library. She asked for beads for Christmas and began making bracelets and necklaces. She asked a local bead shop if she could have a job, but they declined as she was so young. She asked again, and they eventually relented and let her count beads in the back room unpaid. My sister counted beads every Saturday when she wasn't in school. Impressed with her attitude, they offered her a job, and she soon became manager. She went on to study art and fashion at college and is now one of the top purse designers in the world, often flying between Paris, New York, and London. Never let a lack of money stop you from taking a step.

Did you know that 70% of the world's millionaires are self-made? They took a step.

114

A group of 90-year-olds were surveyed. They were asked, if they could live life again, what they would do differently. The answers were varied, but they all agreed on one thing: They would all have taken more risks.

You will never get to your goal if you don't take a step. How much do you want your dream? Is your comfort more important than your dream? If you want to go for your dreams you're going to have to do things that are difficult, tedious, mundane, and scary.

Talent works for risk takers. Talented people often play safe. They're not willing to take a risk. Risk takers are prepared to step out. They are the entrepreneurs. But it's not just about stepping. It's about *consistently* stepping. Going from A to B and having the *discipline* to do so. That's dream achieving in a nutshell!

And never confuse movement with progress. Everyone's moving. Everyone's busy, but not everyone is progressing. Consistently stepping towards your written goal ensures that you are progressing and not just moving, shuffling around on the same few steps of your ladder.

Decide. Do. Succeed. Repeat.
Decide. Do. Succeed. Repeat.
Decide. Do. Succeed. Repeat.
Decide. Do. Succeed. Repeat.
Decide. Do. Succeed. Repeat.
Decide. Do. Succeed. Repeat.
Decide. Do. Succeed. Repeat.
Decide. Do. Succeed. Repeat.
Decide. Do. Succeed. Repeat.
Decide. Do. Succeed. Repeat.
Decide. Do. Succeed. Repeat.
Decide. Do. Succeed. Repeat.
Decide. Do. Succeed. Repeat.
Decide. Do. Succeed. Repeat.
Decide. Do. Succeed. Repeat.
Decide. Do. Succeed. Repeat.
Decide. Do. Succeed. Repeat.
Decide. Do. Succeed. Repeat.
Decide. Do. Succeed. Repeat.

When you prepare to take a step you have four choices.

You have four choices.

You can take no step, a backward step, a small step, or a big step. People who take backward steps say things like, "Oh, I tried investing once. I got burned. Never again!" A lot of people take small steps. That's what most people do. But what would it be like if you took a big step? What would it look like if you did something so radical it would have the effect of massively shifting your life? What if you packed in your job today? Invested everything? Sold your house and moved to help with that African charity this week?

Maybe you're at a time in life when you are not practically able to take a massive step. Whatever your situation, whether it's big or small, you are always able to do something.

If you take a massive step it will cause you problems, but you'll get a big RESULT and you only live once!

CHOOSE TO KEEP STEPPING!

Look up at the top of your ladder. Put your foot on the bottom rung. How do you get from the bottom rung to the top? You keep on stepping!

> Half of all exercise is in your head, so now I just think about it twice as much.

Once, when I owned no rental property, I walked past three derelict, smashed-up shop fronts. I had the thought that one day I could perhaps own one as an investment. Immediately I had the thought, "You need to buy all three!" I thought, "I can't!" Instinctively I changed my thinking to, "How can I? How can I own all three?" I came up with a complicated plan that involved juggling borrowed money and putting down deposits. I also made over sixty-five calls to the owner, asking him to sell them. Eventually he relented, and I converted them into 4-bedroom houses. I climbed a few steps on my dream ladder and I did it by persistence. Sixty calls to one guy is a lot!

Tony Robbins says, "You overestimate what you can do in a year and underestimate what you can do in a decade!" In other words, don't be discouraged by putting a time limit on your dream, just keep on stepping.

The real key to success is therefore *self-discipline.*

Self-discipline is not about saying "no" to thousands of wrong things. Self-discipline is saying "yes" to the one thing you really want. Your "stop doing" list is just as important as your "to do" list.

Do you have the self-discipline? Most people don't. I read books, journal, listen to podcasts, and watch motivational videos. I'm continually being inspired, which gives me the strength to take another step towards my dreams.

Self-discipline is the variable that separates champions from the crowd. Your "why" must be strong. You must have emotional connection to what you really want. How great and important is it? Feel it. Climb the mountain, and feel what it will be like. The "why you want your dream" is what will give you the self-discipline to keep climbing. Being emotionally in tune with what is important keeps you on track. Emotional connection to your dream gives you the discipline to take another step towards it.

Self-discipline sets boundaries that keep you on track. It keeps what you want in and keeps what you want out. It affects your time, your energy, your resources, and your relationships. For instance, you may want to write a book to help single mothers. You set yourself a goal to write every night. Your self-discipline says "no" to having your friends around. You set up time and energy boundaries. Some nights you don't feel like it, but your "why," your desire to help those single mothers keeps you on target.

We live in an entitlement world. "I want it *now* and I deserve it *now!*" So if it's too hard or people can't, then they give up and move on. That's good news for you. You just need an ounce of self-discipline, and you instantly move ahead of most people.

TAKE A STEP

Danny Cahill is America's biggest loser! "I used to look at myself and think, I am horrible, I am a monster, subhuman," he said. Cahill's weight caused him physical pain when walking and climbing stairs. One day, when sleeping in his recliner because he was too heavy to lay down, Cahill realized that if he wanted to lose weight then it was up to him. He went on to lose 239 pounds, moving from 430 to 191 pounds and, by so doing, became "America's biggest loser." How did he do it? *A step at a time!*

Kevin, you are an awfully smart teenager. I think you should jump ahead a couple of pages while I mention social media.

OK.

Good! Peace and quiet for a few pages!

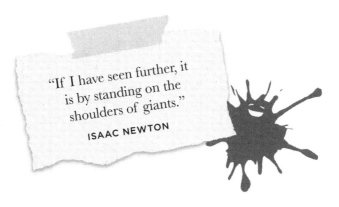

CHAPTER 7

HOW TO SOLVE THIS GIANT PROBLEM!

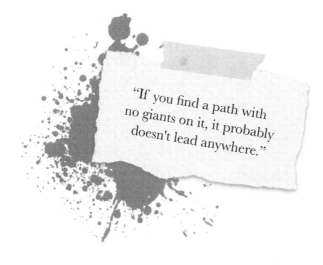

In your pursuit of success you will come across giants.
Giants, although not seen in our natural world, certainly exist. They live in the world of imagination and stand intimidatingly between you and where you want to go.

Giants are defined as "monsters of human appearance, prodigious size and strength." The word *giant*, coined in 1297, derives from the Greek, *gigantes*. In all mythologies giants are featured as primeval creatures associated with chaos and wild nature. Famous giants are found in the stories of David and Goliath, the Giant's Causeway in Ireland, and Jack and the Beanstalk.

Giants thrive off fear. They ooze it! Their purpose is to intimidate and make you feel small. They do not want you to accomplish your goals or dreams, and although you may manage to avoid a few, sooner or later one of them, probably your arch nemesis, will stand directly in your path and there will be a confrontation.

Giants exist is many forms including excuses, procrastination, and confusion. They throw accusations at you like, "What will others say?," "If only people knew what you've done!," and "You'll never be able to do that!" When your giant is stamping, waving his club of intimidation and threatening you with all kinds of accusations, then sense and logic can seem a long way off. Is your dream worth it? Surely you've been here before? Maybe the giant is right? It's probably not worth the fight, energy and effort! The sense of fear can be overwhelming.

> I've started Twittering my opinion every day. I've already got 4 followers: Two police officers, a social worker, and a psychiatrist!

> It was the Giant of Distraction!

> That's got nothing to do with giants.

Here are a few pointers to help you defeat your giant:

1. **Ask yourself the question: What is worse: fear or regret?** Fear is huge. It gets bigger every day, but regret is worse. Regret gets heavier. When you get to the end of your life you will always look back and say, "I wish I'd confronted my giant. I wish I'd gone for my dream. I wish I'd confronted and dealt with that thing. I regret not doing it!"

A lady came up to me and said, "I'm in this awful situation. I know I need to do something. I'm frightened of rocking the boat and of the potential consequences." Although I didn't know the exact situation, I just said, "Regret is worse than fear!" A year later I returned to speak in her place of work. I'd forgotten the conversation until she stepped forward and introduced herself. "I did it," she whispered. "I took action and did it. It was horrible when I did, but now I'm so much happier. You were right. I was frightened to make a change, but I knew I'd always regret it if I didn't. Thank you!"

Fear gets bigger. Regret gets heavier. Decide right now to fight any giant that gets in your way because you do not want to live a life of regret.

2. **Use the right weapon.** You do not defeat giants by growing to be like them or be their size. You defeat a giant by being you. You don't defeat a lying giant by lying. You defeat it by holding to your values. Giants are often defeated by releasing the opposite of what they are. Discouragement is defeated with encouragement. Hate is defeated by love. Procrastination is defeated by hard work. Unkindness is defeated with kindness.

3. **Be prepared.** Every day is a preparation day. Your giant could appear at any time. If you don't work hard today, why will you work hard when the giant comes? Every day counts. Every day is a preparation day. The mundane is a good day because it's a training day.

4. **Don't give up.** You may not win against the giant first time. Keep going. Have courage. Courage is never the absence of fear. It is the decision to show up and fight even though you are afraid. If you don't show up then you lose every time. Have courage, show up, and fight. The giant will eventually fall.

5. **Work out what reward you'll get.** Defeating the biggest giant receives the greatest reward. See your giants, not as something that want to destroy you, but as a necessary part of your journey. See them as a gateway to your dreams. They are a doorway of opportunity. Your promotion and happiness are on the other side. With this mindset you won't run from, but run towards giants. Shift your mindset. Giants are not your problem, they are your promotion.

Defeating giants is a lifetime process, especially if you are a dream achiever and success hunter. Defeating a giant simply gives you permission to fight a bigger one. What's Jack the giant slayer got on you?

There are many types of giants, but here are four that you may encounter. They may appear as an obvious obstacle or more subtly. They may be hiding behind a rung on your ladder or lying sprawled across the path half way up your mountain. Either way, they're nasty and ugly, and you need to defeat them because they stand between you and success.

This is how social media works:

Twitter:	#medefeatinggiants
Facebook:	Thumbs up to me defeating giants
Foursquare:	This is where you learn about me defeating giants
Instagram:	Here's an elevated photo of me defeating a giant
YouTube:	Watch me defeating a giant
LinkedIn:	My skills include giant defeating
Pinterest:	Here's a defeating giant recipe

GIANT #1: THE GIANT OF APATHY

The future you want already exists. It's on another timeline, like a parallel life that you need to step up into. The life you want is there above you, and if you keep doing the things you do now you will never get to it. The way to step up into it is uphill. It takes hard work, and there's a big lazy giant called "Apathy" in the way.

Everyone wants it. Most people talk the talk. Not many people take action. Most people can't be bothered, or at best they give up and are easily distracted. They don't progress; they digress.

"Oh, I don't do schedules! I go with the flow!" Really? Sounds like you have a horizontal schedule playing video games! Set your schedule. Set your compass. Row. Keep checking your charts. If you don't, you'll wake up in a foreign port and wonder how you got there. It's because you didn't have a schedule. You weren't disciplined.

When I had children I had to reinvent my schedule. How much did I want my dream? I had to reset my schedule by resetting my alarm clock to 5 a.m. I rescheduled.

"Schedules are boring. I like random!" You mean you're undisciplined. Create a calendar. Be boring. Actively take a step to your dream every day. Read. Journal. Make a call. Don't let randomness run your life.

Be intentional. Take a step towards your dream on Monday. Take a step on Tuesday. Step on Wednesday. Step deliberately. Stepping isn't luck. Stepping is hard work and takes self-discipline. Step on Thursday. Step on Friday. Step when you feel like it, and step when you don't feel like it until you do feel like it again! Step next week. Step on Sunday, Monday, Tuesday, then guess what? One day you'll wake up and your dreams would have become a reality. You did it by stepping intentionally, each and every day.

Everything good is uphill. It's not easy. Success cannot exist without hard work. You will achieve nothing of value without hard work. Working hard is what successful people do. Your biggest success will come when you swim against the tide. You've got to defeat apathy and start climbing.

A side benefit of hard work is happiness. The harder you work the happier you are with yourself. This new happiness fuels you to take another step.

There is also a law of diminishing returns that you need to be aware of. In any project, big results are often seen in the early stages. As the project sets in, more effort is needed to produce the same results. After early successes in a quest to accomplish your goal, over complacency can happen, and this can be a danger. After one week you are impressed with your weight loss, so you press on with your exercise regime. After six weeks complacency sets in. You are losing weight. It's not so hard. You take an evening off to treat yourself to a dessert. The hard work drops off just at the point when you need to press on to see further weight loss. Suddenly, the big weight loss stops, and with it goes your motivation. Your dream to lose weight fizzles out, and slowly old habits sneak back in and your great project, with all its enthusiasm and hard work, comes to an end and you await the day when something new will kick-start fresh motivation, so you can begin all over again.

"Start tomorrow!" says Giant Apathy. "Tomorrow is when you'll do it!" You have a three second window after his temptation lands. Will you give in or will you take action? Will you go on the power walk or watch the movie? 3...2...1...Too late. Your mind kicks in. The movie was a good one. The beer and chips were delicious. Better try again...tomorrow!

People think I'm lazy because I don't finish what I...

Procrastination doesn't really exist. If I promised to give you a million dollars if you met me at 2 a.m. in the morning, I guarantee you'd be there. You made the goal important enough to push everything else to one side.

What people mean when they put things off is that it's "not important enough." They may also have an insecurity issue and be saying, "Look at me. Notice me. I need attention!"

How do you defeat the Giant of Apathy?

Hard work.

Get emotionally attached to your dream. Make it important enough. Make it so strong that your consistent action and hard work leave the Giant of Apathy crushed and defeated.

Kevin, that section was for you. You're apathetic!

Ask me if I care.

GIANT #2: THE GIANT OF CONFUSION

Which way should you go? What's the right decision? Suddenly, out of the mist looms Giant Confusion. You can't even tell he's there. He's covered in confusion.

Choosing between a good or a bad choice is easy. Choosing between two good choices is harder. They both have pros and cons. Which path should you take? Which of those beautiful people should you go out with? Which top job should you choose? What sunny path should you take? It's a potential life changing choice, so you don't want to get it wrong. You're blindsided by Giant Confusion. He laughs as you struggle with the same issues that go round and round your head.

I love the famous poem by Robert Frost:

• *The Road Not Taken* •

Two roads diverged in a yellow wood,
And sorry I could not travel both
And be one traveler, long I stood
And looked down one as far as I could
To where it bent in the undergrowth;

Then took the other, as just as fair,
And having perhaps the better claim,
Because it was grassy and wanted wear;
Though as for that the passing there
Had worn them really about the same,

And both that morning equally lay
In leaves no step had trodden black.
Oh, I kept the first for another day!
Yet knowing how way leads on to way,
I doubted if I should ever come back.

I shall be telling this with a sigh
Somewhere ages and ages hence:
Two roads diverged in a wood, and I—
I took the one less traveled by,
And that has made all the difference.

ROBERT FROST

Both paths looked good. Did the poet take the wrong or the right one? He doubts he'll come back and knows that his choice will make all the difference. You know you won't come back, so you try to hold on to both options, hoping your difficult decision will resolve itself. You stand paralyzed by Giant Confusion at the crossroads of choice, unable to commit and move forwards.

The Giant of Confusion is defeated by clarity.

Writing things down helps bring clarity. Write the question you are confused by. Then write all the pros and cons of each path. Ask your friends for advice. Write down what they say. Do both paths give you peace?

Then, if you still can't decide, ask yourself this question, "Which one is taking me towards my dream?"

If it's still unclear, then take a step.

The story is told of a city paralyzed by fear. The inhabitants were surrounded by a foreign army and starving to death. Inside the city was a group of lepers. "If we stay here," they said, "We will die, but if we step outside the city we will also die." Both were bad choices. But they decided to take a step, reasoning that if they stayed they were guaranteed to die, but if they went over to the enemy there was a chance to live. On leaving the city they found the enemy had left. They simply had needed to take a step.

When I was twenty-five I couldn't choose between moving to Yorkshire or Australia. I spent countless nights not being able to make up my mind. Eventually my friend said, "You're driving me crazy! Just make a decision!" I chose Australia and a month later was living in Yorkshire! "Analysis paralysis" is always defeated by taking a step. Will you kick the ball to the left or to the right? You'll never know until you move. Just choose a path, step and kick with all your skill and strength.

Clarify your situation. Make the best choice you can. Take a step and don't look back. The right choice is the one you made because you made it. Move on and let the Giant of Confusion fade into the mist behind you.

I think we live in the USA now. Do you know what state?

The state of confusion!

GIANT #3: THE GIANT OF EXCUSES

This giant is more cunning than the others. He comes in several guises, and his appearance is more subtle than other giants. But the reality is, he's a no-good, lying giant, bent double and disguised in sheep's clothing. His words are smooth, seemingly making great sense and easy to swallow and believe. Children call his words *excuses*. Adults call them *reasons*.

His words have a magical quality. They wrap themselves around you, all too easily.

"You're too old!" "You're too young!" "You don't have enough time!" "You have no skill!" "You don't know how!" "You've already tried it once!" "You're not good enough!" "What will others think?"

I will never apologize for who I am.

Why aren't you doing what you want? It may be someone's opinion. Is it a family member? Have a conversation with that person. Don't let someone's opinion get in the way. Why are you so worried about what that person will say?

WHEN PEOPLE GET IT WRONG

Here are what some teachers wrote on their pupils' reports:

"His moral conduct is very satisfactory and
his religious instruction is adequate."

**WRITTEN ABOUT ADOLF HITLER, GERMAN POLITICIAN
ANDLEADER OF THE NAZI PARTY**

"The most difficult boy I have ever had to deal with."

**WRITTEN ABOUT TONY BLAIR,
BRITISH PRIME MINISTER**

"Peter tends to set himself very low targets
which he then fails to achieve."

**WRITTEN ABOUT PETER USTINOV,
WINNER OF TWO ACADEMY AWARDS FOR
BEST SUPPORTING ACTOR, EMMY AWARDS,
GOLDEN GLOBES, BAFTA AWARDS, AND A GRAMMY AWARD**

"Too interested in sport. You can't make a living out of soccer."

**WRITTEN ABOUT GARY LINEKER, INTERNATIONAL
SOCCER SUPERSTAR AND TV PRESENTER**

"She writes indifferently and knows nothing of grammar."
WRITTEN ABOUT CHARLOTTE BRONTE, AUTHOR

"Hopeless. Certainly on the road to failure."
WRITTEN ABOUT JOHN LENNON, MUSICIAN

"Priscilla is suitable for office work."
**WRITTEN ABOUT CILLA BLACK,
TV SHOW HOST AND CELEBRITY**

"He lacks the 'killer instinct' expected of a champion."
**WRITTEN ABOUT TIM HENMAN,
ONE OF BRITAIN'S MOST FAMOUS TENNIS PLAYERS**

"She has a defeatist attitude and she must try
to be less emotional in her dealings with others."
**WRITTEN ABOUT PRINCESS DIANA,
MEMBER OF THE BRITISH ROYAL FAMILY**

Wow! Are you really going to keep listening to what people say about you?

A critic makes people afraid. They want to sabotage your success, even though they think they're doing you a favor. Being a critic is the easiest job in the world. It's one of my pet peeves! It's easy to sit in your armchair critiquing the latest movie. Have you ever made a movie and been through all the hard work it takes to make one? Become a success and earn the right to critique, and even then, do it positively!

Critics are often insecure, often intimidated by your new dream, and so they do everything they can to stop you because your potential success challenges their lifestyle.

"If only you knew my circumstances!"

If only you knew mine! If you wait for things to be perfect then you'll be waiting a long time because they never will be. Unless you go for your dream now you never will.

While you're waiting for the right circumstances someone else is getting the results because they started.

"I'm not good enough. If only you knew!"

Your failures don't make you a failure. They make you experienced. Your divorce doesn't make you a failure. Having no money doesn't mean you are broken. Being sick doesn't mean you can do nothing. Recognize the Giant of Excuses for what he is: a liar who uses half-truths to stop you from climbing.

The truth is you are not stuck. You *do* have options. You *can* take a step. You *do* have resources. You *can* move forwards.

"I haven't got enough time!"

Correct me if I'm wrong, but I think you have twenty-four hours? That's exactly the same amount that the President has to run a country, Richard Branson has to run Virgin, and the British Monarch has to rule an Empire! You have exactly the same amount of time that any successful person has. You're just choosing to fill yours in other ways.

"I don't know what I'm doing!"

Can you count? How did you do that? You learned to. Do you have a passport? You went and got one. Can you play the piano? You practiced. Do you have a driving license? You took lessons. You succeeded by taking action and learning the skills required.

And now you have Google! Let a Filipino 3-year-old teach you how to play the drums. Get a degree online. Learn through podcasts. So much information and type of qualification is available to you and most of it is free! If you don't know what you're doing, then learn it.

"I'm not very creative!"

Yes you are! Most successful people just reinvent the wheel. They take something that exists already and give it a different spin. So can you. There are lots of books on the same subject, all written by a different person but from a different angle. There are lots of coffee houses and lots of businesses. Whatever you choose, just give it your DNA. Improve, change and reinvent it if need be. You don't even have to be super creative. It doesn't have to be different or better, but it needs to be yours!

Do you see how the Giant of Excuses lies to you? Don't be fooled. You can learn it. You do have the time. You don't have to be intimidated by what others think. Now is the perfect time. He's not fooling you anymore. Walk straight through his lying disguise!

GIANT #4: THE GIANT OF MONEY

This Giant doesn't have to be subtle. He's huge and sits laughing, plopped right in the middle of your path. Money is power, and he knows it. Your dream, especially if it's a big one, needs money. He gloats triumphantly. "You can't afford it!" He says, "So you may as well not even start!"

Most people don't have enough money. The poorest to the mega rich would all agree. However, having enough money is not how this giant is defeated.

First, you must release the opposite. The opposite of lack is *generosity*. Start giving! Give to charity. Pay for a stranger's grocery shopping. Send someone a check. Show this Giant that his words don't intimidate you. You break the power of the love of money over your life when you give.

Second, take a step towards him. What can you do? Can you trade something? Save? Ask for money? Get a grant? Take out a loan? Cut expenses? There is *something* you can do. What is it?

The Red
Paperclip House

That paperclip is green!

Shh! It's printed in black and white! They can't tell!

Kyle MacDonald didn't let money get in the way of his dream. He decided to trade items online and keep exchanging them for better things, until he reached his ultimate goal, which was to own his own house.

After one year of internet bartering, which began with a red paperclip and involved fourteen trades, Kyle completed the deal. In 2006 he moved from Vancouver into a two storey, three-bedroom, 1920s farmhouse in Kipling, Canada. The inspiration for the project was a children's game called "Bigger and Better." Growing up in the suburbs of Vancouver, he watched children go door-to-door trying to trade their toys for something more valuable. His trades were:

- Red paperclip
- Pen
- Door knob
- Coleman stove
- Red generator
- An instant party kit
- Bombardier Mach One snowmobile
- Holiday to Yahk
- Cube van
- Recording contract
- A year's free rental in Phoenix, Arizona
- An afternoon with Alice Cooper
- A Kiss snow globe
- A part in the movie *Donna on Demand*

"I didn't know how I was going to get to my goal of house, or how long it would take me, or where the house would be, but I figured that if I kept at it, I would get there in the end," Kyle said.

His house is called, "The Red Paperclip House."

Don't let a lack of money ever stop you from taking a step toward your dream.

Americans love money too much!

How do you know?

I went to watch my first football game. This guy tossed a quarter in the air and then for the next three hours the whole crowd screamed "GET THE QUATER BACK! GET THE QUATER BACK!" ...All for twenty-five cents. Americans are nuts!

Happiness is free, but dreams often do require money. So, how can you practically get the money? You already have the answer; you just need to work it out.

Here are a few trigger questions to help you think:

Every dollar you earn counts. With every dollar you have a choice of where to spend it. Will you give it to the local coffee shop? Will you spend it on a new car? Will you put it into savings or into an asset? Will you put it towards your dream? Every dollar counts and compound interest adds up. Anyone can be a millionaire if they start early and save by compound interest.

Are you tracking your money? People who track their money save 50% more than those who don't.

Are you helping others get what they want? Help others and they'll help you.

Have you written your financial goals? How much do you want to earn? How much do you want to save? What is your total worth? Have you trimmed your expenses? Once you know exactly what you need, you can work on how to get it.

Are you running with your strengths? Did you know that 20% of what you do earns 80% of what you make? Can you spend more time in that 20%?

It is unlikely that saved money will take you to your dream. You need to be creative. Can you invest it? Borrow it? Get financial advice or employ a creative planner? How can you leverage your earned money to make it go further?

Are you automating your pay slips into your savings and putting some aside for your dreams? Those who automate save way more than those who decide to save what's left at the end of their paycheck.

If you want to go from success to success then start from a place of success. What's making you the money now? Isn't that a good place to start from? What's stopping you making more?

What are the lies about money that you believe?

Where are the hungry customers who will buy your idea? Find hungry bait, and you'll catch a lot of fish. What about the fish you've already caught? Are you looking after them? What else can you sell them? Solve their problem. Help people itch their itch, and they'll happily give you their money.

> When I'm famous I'm going to give you lots of my money.

> Thank you. Why?

> Because you're one of the poorest comedians I know!

"You're right," you reply to the Giant. "I don't have the money, but that's not going to stop me. You don't have power over me. I'm still generous. I'm still giving. I'm also saving. I'm asking. I'm borrowing, and I'm investing. I also see that you're getting very uncomfortable and your big lying frame is beginning to shift out my way as I step towards you!"

Giants intimidate. Their power is their seeming size. Their goal is to release fear that immobilizes you in your quest for success.

Be Strong and Courageous!

Watching a hurricane, like the 2017 Hurricane Irma that devastated the Bahamas, the Caribbean, and Florida is not pleasant. Hurricane footage often features flooding, flying roofs, and floating cars. It also shows palm trees bent double in the storm. The interesting thing about palm trees is that they are the only tree that grows in a storm. We can treat giants as a ferocious storm or as an opportunity to help us grow!

Your strength doesn't come from what you can do. Your strength comes from overcoming the things you once thought you couldn't. Giants are therefore one of the *best* things that could happen to you. They are your promotion. Face them. Release the opposite. Slay them. Don't be daunted by your past. Your reward is on the other side.

MY MUM

In 2011 my mother died of cancer. She was a great lady. She loved me through her actions. She sacrificed vacations and many of her dreams so she could provide and give me an education. I stood in silence at the front at her funeral and held a British £2 coin between my fingers. "Do you know what it says round the edge of this coin?" I said softly. "It says, 'Standing on the shoulders of giants!'" My mum was a giant and I'm going to stand on her shoulders to make her proud!"

You have a choice to either let your giants stand on your shoulders or to stand on theirs.

> "Everyone has fallen down or been disappointed in love. Where you truly shine is when you get back up."
>
> SHERRY ARGOV

CHAPTER 8

THE PROVEN FORMULA TO MAKING YOUR DREAMS COME TRUE!

> "I've missed more than 9,000 shots in my career. I've lost almost 300 games. Twenty-six times, I've been trusted to take the game winning shot and missed. I've failed over and over and over again in my life. And that is why I succeed."
>
> MICHAEL JORDAN

There is a mathematical formula to achieving your dream.

Achieving your dream is proportional to the *size of your dream, your desire to achieve it,* and *your ability to overcome disappointment.*

$$\text{Achieving Your Dream} = \text{Size of Dream} + \text{Desire} + \text{Ability to Overcome Disappointment}$$

That makes a lot of sense. If your dream is big then it's harder to accomplish. If it's small then it's easier to achieve. If you are driven, you will stand more of a chance in life than someone who is less driven. What is interesting is the last part, which is your ability to overcome disappointment.

So many people are scared to go for a dream, or they won't do something because they are too afraid of being disappointed.

Disappointment happens to everyone. Will you be disappointed? Yes you will. Guaranteed.

Does disappointment hurt? Yes, it does! Sorry!

Do you have the ability to get up again? Yes, you do.

Do you have the ability to keep getting up again and again? Yes, you do.

Will you get up again? That's the million dollar question: Will your dreams ultimately fail or succeed?

Several years ago I was invited to audition for *Britain's Got Talent*. I spent a lot of time and energy making a promo video, which the studio liked so much that they invited me straight into the quarter-finals. I arrived in Birmingham full of nerves. Huge banners and flags draped over the building. Crowds of adoring fans screamed the names of the British judges, Amanda Holden and Simon Cowell. I entered unknown through a side door.

Yet, I secretly believed that it was my big break. I'd already planned what I was going to do in the semi-final and final. This was my moment of recognition on big stage.

Unfortunately, I was the only contestant that day that they'd sent wrong information to. I had to come back the next day. I re-parked my car (for an extravagant fee), hired a hotel room, told my supporting sister and father they needed to come back and re-motivated myself.

Fortunately, I still believed this was my big break and small mishaps like this happen to superstars like me on their journey to fame and success! Unfazed, I checked in a second time, only to be allotted the death slot, performing at midnight! I waited all day, trying to quench nerves and going over my lines for the ten thousandth time.

Deciding I needed a caffeine buzz before the big moment, I headed to Starbucks, only to spill dark coffee right down the front of my one and only white performing shirt. I had to adapt, and quickly! It was twenty minutes to show time. Like a caffeinated, middle-aged genius I stuck my *Britain's Got Talent* sticker vertically down my shirt, masking 90% of the accident. Simon Cowell would be pleased with my creativity.

I was bustled through the remaining contestants: a near-naked dance troupe, a flock of clucking chickens, a drag-queen, and a giant robot. I was truly on *Britain's Got Talent!* After shaking back-stage super celebrities Ant's and Dec's hands, I made my way, in silence, across the vast stage to the rather lonely looking microphone.

Four judges stared at me. I'd seen them on TV and now they were talking to me! "What's your name?" "How old are you?" "What do you do?" A few more questions and I started my act.

"RRRRRRRRRRRRRRR!" The buzzer sounded. It was loud. Simon Cowell had pushed it. "Stop! Stop! Stop!" he monotoned. "Do you do anything else?" I was thrown. Shaken. This wasn't how it was supposed to be. I flustered. I stammered. I pulled out an emergency puppet I'd not practiced with. I got through. It wasn't good.

I got two "yes" votes and two "no" votes. It wasn't enough. I remember the sense of puzzlement that came over me. This wasn't the way that it was supposed to be! In front of 2,000 people and another 12 million on camera, I made my painful exit— at midnight!

My mind spun. I was embarrassed. It had gone wrong. That wasn't supposed to happen. I exited down the back stairs. A group of audience members recognized me and said they liked it, but I knew they were just being nice.

An hour later I lay in my hotel room. For three hours my head spun. I couldn't sleep. A barrage of thoughts hit me: "Who did Simon Cowell think he was? He didn't understand!" My dream was shattered. The overwhelming sense of disappointment was enormous.

Will you ever be disappointed? If you are daring enough to take a step towards your dreams then yes, you will. Do you want to go through life and never be disappointed, protecting your heart from ever being hurt and let down? Then get ready for a very boring life. Ultimately you may avoid disappointment, but you will end your life with the ultimate disappointment—not making the most of it, because you were afraid to take any risks.

You will fall and be disappointed. Guaranteed. So the real question isn't *if* you will be disappointed, it's *how long* will you stay down before you get back up? Most people eventually pull themselves up again, but they spend a lot of wasted time doing it. The trick is to be able to bounce back immediately. Get over the pain and rejection. Don't take it so personally. Realize it's a part of dream achieving. Embrace the lessons you just learned. Add it in your wisdom bank.

Most people's disappointment graph looks like this:

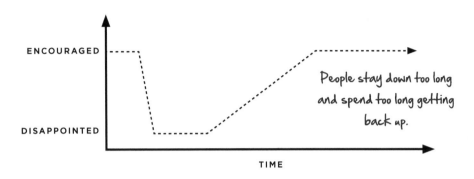

But you want your graph to look like this:

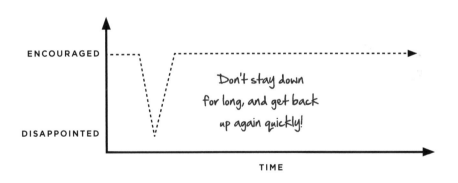

It's not *if* you slip off the rung of your ladder. It's *how fast* will you get back up on it again.

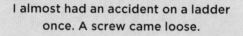

I almost had an accident on a ladder once. A screw came loose.

Did you fall?

No, but my wooden leg fell off!

GRANDMA CHA

Grandma Cha holds an unusual world record. She has failed her driving test 959 times!

This 69-year-old Korean woman, who lives alone in the mountain-ringed village of Cinchona, failed her written test once a day, five days a week, for three years! Grandma Cha, whose name, ironically, is Korean for "vehicle," said she had always envied people who could drive, but it was not until she was in her 60s that she got around to trying for a license. "I wanted to get a driver's license so I could take my grandchildren to the zoo."

Every day at 4 a.m. she pored over her well-worn test preparation books. "She could read and write words phonetically, but she could not understand most of the terminology," said her teacher. For each of her 960 tests, she had to pay $5 in application fees.

On her 960th try, she achieved a passing grade of 60 out of 100. Grandma Cha had given new meaning to the Korean boxing saying, *Sajeonogi*, meaning, "Knocked down four times, but rising up five." On her wall she had posted a handwritten and misspelled note that read, "Never give up!"

Passing a driving test probably doesn't seem like such a big dream to most people. The ladder wasn't very high. It only had a couple of rungs, but to Grandma Cha that first rung, needing to pass her written exam, was a very slippery and difficult one. But she just kept getting back on her ladder again and again, and in the end she got to her goal.

Life doesn't ever quite turn out how you expect. I love funny stories, and this one always makes me laugh:

A SHOCKING STORY!

Last weekend I saw something at *Larry's Pistol & Pawn Shop* that sparked my interest. The occasion was our 15th anniversary and I was looking for something special for my wife, Julie. What I came across was a 100,000 volt, purse-sized Taser. The effects of the Taser were supposed to be short lived, with no long-term adverse effect on your assailant.

WAY TOO COOL! Long story short, I bought the device and brought it home. I loaded it with two AAA batteries and pushed the button. Nothing! I was disappointed. I learned, however, that if I pushed the button AND pressed it against a metal surface at the same time, I'd get the blue arc of electricity darting back and forth between the prongs. AWESOME! (I have yet to explain to Julie how the burn spot is on the face of her microwave got there!)

Alone with this new toy, I thought to myself that it couldn't be all that bad with only two tiny batteries, right? I sat in my recliner with my trusting cat, Gracie, looking at me intently while I read the directions, thinking that I really needed to try this thing out on a flesh and blood target. I confess that I did think about zapping Gracie, but thought better of it. If I was going to give this to my wife to protect herself against a mugger, I wanted some proper assurance that it was the real deal!

So, there I sat wearing shorts, a tank top, reading glasses perched delicately on the bridge of my nose, directions in one hand, and the taser in the other. The directions said a one-second burst would "shock and disorient your assailant," a two-second burst would cause "muscle spasms and minor loss of bodily control," a three-second burst would purportedly make your assailant "flop on the ground like a fish out of water," and any burst longer than three seconds would be "wasting the batteries."

I looked at the tiny device, measuring a few inches long, half an inch in circumference, loaded with two really tiny batteries and thought to myself, 'No possible way!' What happened next is almost beyond description, but I'll do my best!

I'm sitting there alone, with Gracie looking on, with her head to one side as if to say, "DO NOT DO IT!" Reasoning that a brief burst from such a tiny device could hardly hurt, I decided to give myself a one-second burst just for the heck of it. I touched the prongs to my naked thigh and pushed the button.

"WHAT THE...WEAPONS OF MASS DESTRUCTION... @$%&@£*%!!!!!!"

An enormous body builder ran through the door, picked me up, and body slammed me on the carpet over and over again. I vaguely recall waking in the fetal position, tears streaming from my eyes, body soaking wet, both nipples on fire, testicles gone, my left arm tucked backwards under my body and violent tingling shooting through both legs! Gracie was making strange meows from the safety of a distant dining chair in her attempt to avoid being slam-dunked by my body flopping all over the room!

Note: If you ever feel compelled to mug yourself with a Taser, one note of caution: there is no such thing as a gentle, one second burst! You will not let go of that @%$£@& thing until it is dislodged from your hand by a violent thrashing on the floor. A three-second burst would be considered conservative!

A minute or so later (time was relative at that point), I collected my wits and surveyed the landscape. My bent reading glasses were in the fireplace. The recliner was upside down and several feet from where it originally was. My triceps, right thigh and nipples still twitched uncontrollably. My face felt like it had been shot-up with *Novocain,* and my bottom lip weighed eighty-eight pounds! I had no control over the drooling. My hair smelt of smoke, and I think my pants needed changing, though I was too numb to be fully sure!

Maybe your disappointments have been self-inflicted. Maybe they were out of your control. Or maybe you did your absolute best, but you've been disappointed yet again. I'm sorry. I really know that feeling. It's so painful.

Small consolation as it is, disappointment actually stops your competition getting where you want to go. If there was no disappointment then everyone else would be at the top of your mountain already.

NEVER, NEVER GIVE UP!

In the midst of World War II, in a time of being bombed nightly, Winston Churchill, Prime Minister of Great Britain, stood up and gave a four minute speech that changed history. "Never give in, never give in, never, never, never, never—in nothing, great or small, large or petty—never give in, except to convictions of honor and good sense."

Inventor Thomas Edison holds the world record for over a thousand patents. He viewed failure as success. In his quest to invest the lightbulb he failed over 10,000 times and was quoted as saying, "I have not failed; I have just found 10,000 ways that won't work!"

At the age of thirteen, surfing prodigy Bethany Hamilton lost her entire left arm to a tiger shark just off the coast of Kauai. While most would give up on their dreams, Bethany didn't. Her dream was to be a professional surfer. She was back in the water a month after the incident.

Babe Ruth was one of the greatest hitters in the history of major league baseball. In 1927 he hit sixty home runs, a record that stood for forty-three years. He had a lifetime record of 714 home runs. He was known as the "Home Run King." However, he held a lifetime strikeout record of 1,330. He was also the "King of Strikeouts. He was not afraid to strike out.

"Everyone is a fighter until they get hit!" said Mike Tyson.

Disappointment hurts. So what are you going to do when you do get hit? What are you going to do when your experiment fails or you strike out or you get bitten? Are you going to give up or get up? Never, never, never give up! Life is not just about being the right person in the right place at the right time, but also about being the wrong person in the wrong place at the wrong time, and not giving up!

SUSAN'S STORY

Susan was born in 1961 in a small town in Scotland, daughter to Irish immigrants. At birth she was deprived of oxygen, causing brain damage. She was diagnosed with mild brain trauma, which caused learning difficulties and made her an easy target for bullies at school. She was mocked, abused, and ridiculed.

"Simple Susie" felt isolated and misunderstood. Her dream to sing was nonexistent, and having failed at school she got a job helping in a kitchen. Hearing about a singing audition she traveled to Glasgow, only to be rejected because of her looks.

Her father died, and her mother sunk into deep depression. Susan used up all her savings to pay for a professional demo tape which she sent to television studios, talent competitions, and record companies. She didn't receive a single reply.

Her sister and mother both then died, causing her severe depression. Finally, in honor of her mother, she decided to try one final singing audition on *Britain's Got Talent* on April 11, 2009. Simon Cowell rolled his eyes as Susan Boyle stepped on stage, but the moment she opened her mouth and began singing "I Dreamed a Dream," all the judges were speechless.

Susan Boyle went on to become a superstar, singing for the Pope, the Queen, and President Obama. Today the singer's estimated net worth is $33 million, yet she humbly chooses to live in her mother's end-of-terrace ex-council house.

Can you get up one more time?

The opposite of disappointment is appointment. Your dream is appointed to you. The moment you wrote it, it became yours. How much do you want it? It's your dream. Stamp it on your heart. Stamp it on your thoughts. Stamp it on your world. Take my hand and get up again.

You *are* appointed to succeed!

That chapter may have seemed small and insignificant, but it was actually profound and a big deal.

Like me when I come on stage!

It's not about you!

I'm disappointed.

Get used to it!

CHAPTER 9

YES YOU CAN!

En-cour-age-ment. *Noun.* **"The action of giving someone support, confidence, or hope."**

At the 1992 Olympic Games in Barcelona, sprinter Dereck Redmond's hamstring gave way in the middle of his semi-final. While most athletes would have given up, Dereck picked himself up and in tears hobbled on, completely out of the race. Suddenly, pushing officials to one side, a man burst onto the track, threw his arm around Dereck and urged him on. Dereck cried on his father's shoulder as together they crossed the finish line together.

Encouragement is life to our dreams. We can't get enough of it.

 Yawning is contagious. Researchers at the University of Nottingham in the UK looked at what happens in our brains to trigger that response. They found that contagious yawning is a common form of *echophenomena*, an automatic imitation of someone else's words or actions.

You probably yawned just looking at the picture.

Friends, like yawning, are infectious. It is essential you surround yourself not with friends, but with *great* friends and *great* resources that keep you encouraged as you climb your ladder to success.

A friend listens.
A good friend cares.
A great friend encourages.
A hero inspires.

> I'll do my best to inspire, but I'm only human. Kevin, what are you?

> A teenager.

HOW MANY FRIENDS?

A gym instructor was once asked by a student how many friends he should have. The teacher pointed to the ceiling. "Touch it!" she said.

The student scratched his head, "But it's too high. I can't!"

"Ask a friend, maybe they'll help," smiled the teacher.
The student called another student and stood on their shoulders. "I still can't reach."

"Don't you have more friends?"

The student called more friends and soon everyone was building a live pyramid. But the pyramid crumbled and the students crashed painfully to the floor. "Now I understand," the student said, "I need a lot of friends!

"Yes," the teacher agreed, "A lot. I hope you find one smart enough to use a ladder!"

You don't need a lot of friends, just one smart enough to do life well with. Who's encouraging you? Who inspires you? How are you getting your encouragement?

THE DIFFERENCE FACTOR

The difference between who you are today and who you'll be in ten years is determined by two factors:

First, it is determined by the people you spend time with. Surround yourself with losers, and you'll become a loser. Surround yourself with chess players, and you'll become good at chess. Surround yourself with positive people, and you'll become positive. Get the wrong people out of your social circles and the right people in. Stop going to places where losers are. Start going to places where winners go.

But what about the people you can't change? Usually family! You still love them, but what they say sometimes isn't always the most helpful or positive. Set boundaries. Don't answer the phone at inconvenient times. Don't spend so much time with them. Change the conversation to positive subjects. If they cross your boundary then withdraw. If they "play ball," engage. They'll soon get your rules. If they want to spend time with you, then they need to play by your rules.

The second major factor that determines who you'll be in ten years is determined by the books you read. The average person reads one book a year. A top business executive reads a book a week. That's fifty-two books a year. They are filling themselves up with fifty-two times as much knowledge, inspiration and motivation than the average person. They are hanging out with fifty-two successful people every year. They are soaking themselves in the wisdom and expertise of fifty-two genius minds.

In ten years the average person would have read ten books. Some of those will probably be mindless novels. The top executive would have read 520 books. Which one is going to be bigger, better, and more improved? Which person is going to have the knowledge to implement actions to get amazing results? Which one bucks the majority? Which one do you want to be?

Of course, reading a book a week has a cost. Are you prepared to get up twenty minutes earlier? Are you prepared to swap your music for a book? Are you prepared to turn your TV off half-an-hour early? Being great and being awesome comes at a price. Are you willing to pay it?

As a teen, Dan was questioned by his friends. "Do you *really* want to spend that much time reading?" Ask him now. Dan Barber is a celebrated chef, dedicated farmer, and a leading revolutionary in the food industry.

Many of my heroes are too successful and too famous for me to access, but I can read their books. I can spend quality time reading their stories, obtaining their wisdom, and hanging out with them for a few hours every day. I love spending time with the rich and famous!

Immerse yourself in encouragement. Stick notes on your mirror. Put pictures on your fridge. Change your screensaver. Start a positive-only journal. Order a new book. Change the channel. Ramp up the music. Turn off the radio. Download an inspirational podcast to run to. Subscribe to a motivational YouTube channel. That's ten ways to pump new encouragement into you.

Be the flamingo in the flock of pigeons.

Choose three of these and commit to doing them today. Three simple goals. Completing these small goals will boost your esteem and confidence, naturally encouraging you further. Achieving any type of goal encourages you.

Difficult roads often lead to beautiful destinations.

A little progress each day adds up to big results.

When it's dark, look for stars!

YES YOU CAN!

GO ON ADVENTURES TO FIND WHERE YOU TRULY BELONG.

Maybe it won't work out, but seeing if it does will be the best adventure ever.

How would you encourage yourself? Write a Post-it Note to yourself. What do you need to hear?

MOVE IT!

Motivation is a real force. It pushed you forwards. Motivation means "to move."

This book's goal is to encourage you to move from one place to another; to move you from apathy to action, to move you from mundane to excitement, to move you from poor to good, and then to motivate you from good to great.

Motivational guru Zig Ziglar said, "People often say that motivation doesn't last. Well, neither does bathing—that's why we recommend it daily!" Motivation is your fuel. You can't get enough of it. So many people start a project but then give up and fade away. They run out of motivation. You have to stay fueled up or your plane will nosedive, and you won't ever land on the runway of success.

Motivation can either be positive or negative. Negative motivation is fueled by fear. The fear of what others will think if you fail. The fear of having to stay in the same overly large body. The fear of not being able to pay the mortgage. The fear of getting to the end of your life and feeling you've wasted it.

> Never let anyone treat you like a purple Starburst. You are a yellow Starburst!

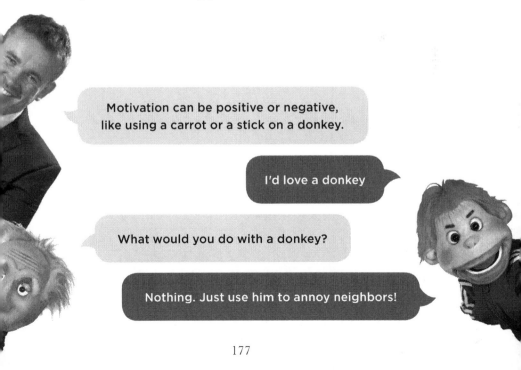

Motivation can be positive or negative, like using a carrot or a stick on a donkey.

I'd love a donkey

What would you do with a donkey?

Nothing. Just use him to annoy neighbors!

Positive motivation pulls you forwards. It is the desire to get recognition for your success, the mental picture of the body you want, the feeling you will get because of increased self-esteem, and the future feeling of success.

My dad's motivating factor is my sister. (He loves me too, but he loves my sister!) If I ask my dad to paint a picture he will consider it. If I ask him to paint a picture for my sister he will get excited and happily paint one. It's the same action, but one route is fueled by heart motivation.

I can dance, sing, and tell you motivational stories all day in an attempt to inspire you. Some may momentarily work and some will come across as hype, but the moment I tap into your dreams, I won't have to motivate you. Your dream will do that for me.

Great leaders don't spend countless resources trying to motivate people to stay on their bus. They set clear goals. Customers, employees, and followers don't need encouragement to stay on the bus if everyone is happy where the bus is going.

Your ultimate motivation and encouragement is your dream. Surround yourself with great resources and great friends and keep focused on the dream.

Positive motivation is like going jogging and there's a hot girl in front!

Negative motivation is when there's a creepy guy behind!

YES I CAN!

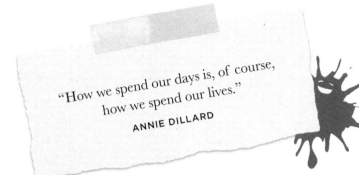

"How we spend our days is, of course, how we spend our lives."

ANNIE DILLARD

CHAPTER 10

NOW YOU CAN HAVE THEM!

"Yesterday is history. The past is a mystery. Today is a gift, and that is why it is called *the present!*"

KUNG FU PANDA

In the movie, *Dead Poets Society*, school teacher John Keating, played by Robin Williams, inspires his class of students to live life with passion. In one scene he tells them to look at black and white photographs of past students.

"They're not that different from you, are they?" He explains. "Same haircuts. Full of hormones, just like you. Invincible, just like you feel. The world is their oyster. They believe they're destined for great things, just like many of you; their eyes are full of hope, just like you. Did they wait until it was too late to make from their lives even one iota of what they were capable? Because, you see gentlemen, these boys are now fertilizing daffodils."

The boys stare in spellbound silence as John Keating whispers, "But if you listen real close, you can hear them whisper their legacy to you. Go on, lean in. Listen, you hear it? *Carpe diem...*Hear it? *Carpe diem!* Seize the day. Make your lives extraordinary!"

So many people live for the future, "When that happens!" So many people live in the past, "I wish that could happen again!" But so few people are happy in the now. Yet now is all we ever have.

HOW MANY DO YOU HAVE?

Have you ever numbered your days?

Let's say (and don't complain to me if you don't make it), that you're going to live to eighty. The average human age is nearer seventy-five, but you're special and never eat desserts, so let's just say eighty!

Let's also take an example age of you being thirty-five. If you're younger, congratulations and if you're older, congratulations! That means you have already lived 35 x 365 = 12,775 days. You have 45 x 365 = 16,425 days remaining.

But let's take into account that a third of that time is sleeping. That's 10,950 days remaining. The average person spends around seventeen minutes a day in the bathroom. On average we spend sixty-eight minutes a day eating, thirty-five minutes on food preparation and cleanup, two hours and thirty-six minutes watching TV on weekdays and a monster three hours and twenty-one minutes watching TV on weekend days, while the average time on housework is forty-nine minutes.

Don't forget the seven minutes complaining at your spouse for not helping more!

You also need to take into account vacations, coffee breaks, and the killer commute. Average commuting time to work is twenty-seven minutes—one way. That's nine days a year commuting!

Oh, and don't forget social media. The average daily time on YouTube is forty minutes, Facebook is thirty-six minutes, Snapchat is twenty-five minutes, Instagram is fifteen minutes, and Twitter is one minute. Over a lifetime, that's eight months on Instagram, fourteen months on Snapchat, a year and seven months of Facebook, just under two years on YouTube, and a very conservative eighteen days on Twitter. The average person will spend five years and four months of their life on social media!

Have you ever complained you've not got enough time?

By the time you extract the social media, commuting, eating, bathroom breaks, watching TV, and housework you have 4,916 working days left. That's assuming you are thirty-five and you are going to work until you are eighty. If you're forty-five and want to retire at sixty, then you have nearer 2,000 working days left.

Oh, I forgot to say, you'll also spend two weeks of your life waiting at traffic lights!

What are you going to do with your remaining days? Stop wasting them! Making the decision to get rid of your TV instantly gives you two-and-a-half more years of life!

"I don't have time to read a book!"

I don't believe you!

Time is the most precious commodity and it passes by every second.

Interestingly, if you look back over your life, how many days can you actually remember? Possibly not more than 100 days. You can probably remember a few fun birthdays, some special occasions, and a couple of momentous events. So what happened to the other 12,675 days? Where have they gone? Those days have been essential. They've been the making of you. In those days you "did life," with all its ups and downs. They have made you the person you are today.

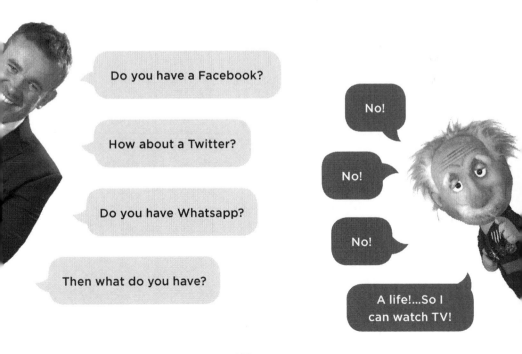

BE ON TIME!

After twenty-five years, Father Williams was saying his goodbyes at his retirement dinner. A prominent member in the congregation, a leading politician, had been asked to give a short speech, but was very late. So the priest took it upon himself to fill the time, and stood up to the microphone.

He said, "I remember the first confession I heard here twenty-five years ago, and it worried me so much. It is still the worst I ever heard. The man confessed that he'd stolen money from parents and employers. He'd had several affairs. He'd taken hard drugs, committed violent acts and was a compulsive liar. However, I soon realized that this sad man was an exception in this parish with its wonderful people."

At this point the politician arrived, apologized for being late and took the stage. He pulled his speech from his pocket and started, "I'll always remember when Father Williams first came to our parish. I was the first person that he heard in confession."

It's good to be on time!

TWO TYPES OF TIME

Greek has two words for time. One is *chronos*, meaning "times," and one is *kairos*, meaning "seasons." It's important you know the difference.

The word "chronology" derives from *chronos*. These are the times when we do the mundane of life. We go about our business and create habits.

Kairos is a specific time. It is the big moment or the big event.

You need to recognize the difference. Everyone wants the *kairos* moment. We all want success, to achieve a goal and stand on a mountain, yet we must understand that those are fleeting moments, special and sporadic, and that real life is made up of *chronos* days. If your happiness is dependent on a *kairos* moment then you won't have much of it! You need to be appreciative and embrace the mundane of life because real happiness is found in *chronos* times.

Don't underestimate the mundane. The mundane is what makes you a champion. Unless you can live well in *chronos* days, you won't be ready when your *kairos* opportunity arrives. The employee who faithfully comes to work on time and does a good job is the one who is ready for their *kairos* promotion when it suddenly arises.

In *chronos* times you learn important things, like how to overcome giants, improve attitude, increase skills, obtain knowledge, be excellent, etc. If you don't learn these in *chronos* times, then you won't be ready when your big moment comes.

Take traffic lights as an example. You could live frustrated and impatient for two weeks of your life stuck at traffic lights! Or, you could leverage them to your advantage. Use the time stopped to be thankful. Make red lights a trigger to remind you to smile. Say a prayer for someone. Shifting your mind into a state of thankfulness is proven to improve creativity by 20% and it removes stress. Traffic lights are now your friend! Red to stress, green to dream! *Chronos* them! Shift gear into awesome!

JOE FOWLER

Joe Fowler helped design a couple of battleships that were used in the Second World War.

> How do you sink a ship designed by a public committee?

> How?

> Put it in water!

188

NOW YOU CAN HAVE THEM!

He attended the United States Naval Academy, earned a degree in naval architecture and went on to become an Admiral. He retired from the navy in 1948. A short time after retiring Joe received a phone call.

"Joe, I hear you designed battleships. If you designed a battleship, could you come and design for me? My name is Walt Disney. I have this idea called 'Disneyland!'"

In a moment, all Joe Fowler's hard work, all his *chronos* moments turned into one giant *kairos* moment. He was hired as construction boss for the whole Disneyland project and then ran it for ten years before retiring again. He came out of retirement a second time to assist with the construction of Disney World before eventually hanging up his pen at the age of ninety-nine! His famous catchphrase was, "Sure can!" He had a great attitude. When interviewed later in life, he was asked why he was still working. He replied, "You don't have to die until you want to!"

His insatiable desire for life and his dream to build pulled him forwards into life.

In his honor, the dock in Disneyland, located across from Haunted Mansion, is named Fowler's Harbor, and one of the ferries to the Magic Kingdom is named Admiral Joe Fowler.

WHAT IF?

You are never too old to set another goal or to dream a new dream. If it was guaranteed that you would live to 100, how would that change the way you live? What if you lived to 100? You'd probably think, "Wow! I have so much time! Why am I just aiming to retire at fifty-five? There's so much I could do!"

With young children, I get up at 5 a.m. to work, sometimes earlier. If I don't I won't get started until after school run. The routine works great for me because I'm up, fresh and ready to help my wife at 7 a.m. when the kids get up. If you're not maxing your time, then you sure aren't maxing your life! Live an awesome day, and you'll live an awesome life.

If you ever ask someone why they are up so early, it's a sure sign that you're not a winning player. "But Marc, you don't understand, I'm a night owl!" I don't really buy that, but that's fine. It just means you've built an unhealthy habit of staying up late. If that's the way you do life, that's fine. Just utilize your time creatively, rather than bowing to the TV god.

THE TV GOD

A realtor once came to value my property. He looked round my house and said, "Where's the TV?" I said, "I don't have one!" He looked at me suspiciously and said, "In twenty-five years of valuing houses, you're only the second person I've come across that hasn't got a TV. I find it kind of *spooky!*"

I find it kind of spooky how so many people bow to their TV god in Lounge Temple!

Since the realtor's visit, I have acquired a TV for my children, but their TV time is limited. I love them too much to use my TV as a convenient babysitter because I'm too lazy to father them, or too work orientated to spend time with them, or too apathetic to let them waste their teens in an armchair. Our TV has an on/off switch and I have the self-discipline to use it.

I value my time, and I value my family.

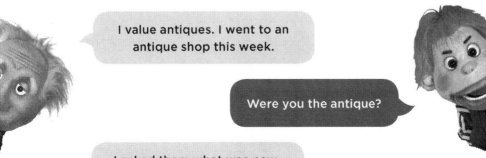

I value antiques. I went to an antique shop this week.

Were you the antique?

I asked them what was new. They said "nothing!"

MAXIMIZE YOUR TIME

Do things faster. What should take a year, do in a month. What should take a week, do in a day. I wanted to renovate three old stone barns. It was a big job that, on some days, involved a team of fourteen people. My goal was to convert them into deluxe accommodation in a two-year timeframe. My good friend gave me a mind shift. "Why waste all that time? Do them in a year!" I recalculated. It took me eighteen months. He saved me six months of life. Compress your time.

Old ways don't open new doors.

STOP BEING BUSY!

Don't live busy. That's western culture's newest problem. "How are you?" "I'm fine, but I'm so *busy!*" We all have 24/7. Do you want to live busy or do you want to live the life you want?

A manager called me after one of my lectures. She said, "I was just about to do all my office work when I remembered what you said about putting what's important ahead of my 'to-do list.'" She went on to tell me how she'd pushed her work to one side and sat on her sofa with her nine-year-old daughter instead. After ten minutes her daughter said, "Mum, that's the longest hug we've ever had!"

Put the important in your day FIRST. Stop being so busy!

STOP!

When did you last stop before getting in your car to look up at the sky, just for a few seconds, before rushing somewhere?

When did you last stop and appreciate how your thumb moves when you wish it to?

When did you last walk through a graveyard and appreciate life?

Don't do that one too often!

When did you last stop and light a candle? Light one tonight for half-an-hour. Put a pen and notepad next to you when you do, so you can jot down interrupting thoughts to help you stay in the moment.

Breathe.

Dream.

Think.

Gandhi changed the world by taking one day off a week just to think. This one action alone will change your life. You are a genius. You already have the answers. You've just been letting your time get cluttered up.

Or maybe you're happy to let your time get cluttered up, so you don't *have* to think?

Huh?

HOW DO YOU PARK YOUR SHOPPING CART?

Your groceries are in the car. You close your trunk, and then what do you do with your cart? Do you leave it? After all, you'd be doing the shopping cart team a favor by keeping them in work! Maybe you play a game and give it a good shove and hope it reaches that distant cart bay? Maybe you stick it back at a weird angle, after all, everyone else has!

Show me how someone parks their shopping cart, and I'll show you how they live life.

BE EXCELLENT!

Excellence is striving for *quality*. A focus on excellence means we take time, work hard, and think carefully about a project or activity. Excellence lets us take pride in our accomplishments. We are guided by an ideal, and we do our best to make it a reality.

With excellence we must also have balance, because when we seek excellence in one area, we risk neglecting other priorities. Excellence doesn't mean being perfect; it means using our abilities to their fullest. A commitment to excellence brings us closer to an enjoyment of life, a bettering of the world, and an attainment of our dreams.

Be excellent at whatever you do. Be excellent in the *chronos* of life. Be excellent when no one else is looking or cares. Be on time. Walk a bit faster. Stand up straighter. Smile. Dress well. Shine your shoes. Don't just clean your plate away, tidy the whole table. Buy their food too! Be excellent in everything and definitely park your shopping cart well.

Excellence gives you energy! If you're a teacher and you need to put up a wall display, then make it excellent. Don't cut corners. Make it the best display you can. Do research. Buy materials. Maybe it will be noticed and maybe it won't. But you know. You did a job of excellence. Your self-esteem goes up. You have more energy for life.

Excellence attracts promotion. Be at your desk five minutes early. Have your coffee made and get working. Do the same at lunchtime and finish five minutes after colleagues at the close of day. You will be giving your boss twenty minutes extra every day. Most people steal that time. You are now twenty-three days a year more valuable to your boss! Who do you think is going to get noticed when it's time for promotion?

Be excellent with your time. What's the worst moment in your week? Turn it into your best one! Have pizza night on Monday. Have T.G.I.M. "Thank Goodness It's Monday!" A teacher emailed me. "I love that!" she said, "I now have T.G.I.S.E. 'Thank Goodness It's Sunday Evening!' It's my family night. We have steak. I've turned my worst moment into my best one!" Be excellent with your time.

Kathy Kreiner proudly stood on the podium listening to Canada's national anthem. She had skied the race of her life to snatch Olympic gold in the giant slalom and become a national hero, fulfilling her childhood dream at the age of eighteen. She went on to become a sport psychologist whose message was to motivate her clients to excellence. "Olympic gold may not be for everyone," she said, "but excellence is."

> Excellence is not being the best. It's doing your best!

WHAT'S YOUR VALUE?

A beggar shouted to a passing king for money. The king stopped his carriage and pulled a gold coin from his purse.

"Your majesty," whispered his deputy, "This gold coin is far too much for this poor beggar. He would be more than content with a single penny coin!"

"Yes," said the King. "That may be his value, but it's not mine. What's good enough for him is not good enough for me!"

He knew his worth. He was King.

When you give to a street beggar, do you give to make yourself feel less guilty? When you give to a church or charity, do you give to the need, because you were asked, or do you give based on your value?

When I visit a coffee shop and use the bathroom I always try and clean it up and make it a little nicer than it looked before. Does anyone care or will anyone ever know? I will.

I have a value of excellence.

VALUES

Have you ever worked out your values?

Let's do a quick test. Pick your top 5 values from this list:

☐ Authenticity
☐ Achievement
☐ Adventure
☐ Autonomy
☐ Balance
☐ Beauty
☐ Boldness
☐ Compassion
☐ Citizenship
☐ Community
☐ Competency
☐ Contribution
☐ Creativity
☐ Curiosity
☐ Determination
☐ Excellence
☐ Fairness
☐ Faith
☐ Friendship
☐ Fun
☐ Growth
☐ Happiness
☐ Honesty
☐ Humor
☐ Influence
☐ Inner Harmony
☐ Justice
☐ Kindness

☐ Knowledge
☐ Leadership
☐ Learning
☐ Love
☐ Loyalty
☐ Meaning
☐ Openness
☐ Optimism
☐ Peace
☐ Pleasure
☐ Popularity
☐ Recognition
☐ Reputation
☐ Respect
☐ Responsibility
☐ Security
☐ Self-Respect
☐ Service
☐ Spirituality
☐ Stability
☐ Success
☐ Status
☐ Trustworthiness
☐ _____
☐ _____
☐ _____
☐ _____
☐ _____

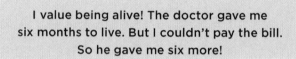

I value being alive! The doctor gave me six months to live. But I couldn't pay the bill. So he gave me six more!

On your journey to success, never compromise your values. They're what you live by. Embrace them. They give you energy. If your value is freedom, and you're stuck in an office, you'll be miserable. If your value is family, and you're spending too much time away, you'll be unhappy. Your values energize you towards your dreams.

THE RECIPE FOR SUCCESS

Massimo looked at his empty restaurant. His dream to be a successful chef was in ruins. He had risked his life savings and stuck to his values to create a type of food that had never been seen before. But others hadn't seen his food that way. The local newspaper had ridiculed his restaurant decor and food, and the locals had rejected him. He now loitered on bankruptcy. However his wife, his one true friend, urged him to try just once more. "Unless you do," she said, "You will always live with the regret!"

A short time after, in April 2001, a leading Italian food critic got stuck in traffic, caused by construction. He diverted through Massimo's town and ended up eating in his restaurant. Two days later the national food magazine ran an article apologizing to Massimo for not eating his superb postmodern food or for visiting his restaurant sooner! Critics took notice and soon his food was receiving rave reviews.

Massimo Bottura won best chef of the year. His Michelin three star restaurant *Osteria Francescana* in Modena, Italy is now voted the third best restaurant in the world! He's famous now for dishes such as "Oops! I dropped the lemon tart," "An eel swimming up the Po river," and "Chocolate, chocolate, chocolate!"

All Massimo's *chronos* moments were forgotten in one glorious *kairos* moment. Massimo got up one more time. His food is adored and respected by the whole of Italy, and now even the locals love his restaurant— when they can get in!

Max your time by being excellent and sticking to your values in *chronos* times. You'll then live happy and be ready for your big *kairos* moment.

"Oops! I dropped the lemon tart."

And always park your shopping cart well. You never know when someone will notice.

Do you see the potential?

"You have to think anyway.
So why not think big?"

DONALD TRUMP

THE BIG
BONUS CHAPTER

MAKE YOUR DREAMS
HAPPEN FASTER!

"Your beliefs become your thoughts,
and your thoughts become your actions."

M. K. GANDHI

You can think big, or you can think small.

Life's too short to be small, so why not set a HUGE AUDACIOUS GOAL? So what if you fail? At least you will have the satisfaction that you tried. You gave life your best shot. The opposite is far sadder—to sit in your armchair with the niggling thought that you always played safe, never knowing what you were capable of, and always wondering what could have been.

THE GENIUS IN YOU!

In 1983 American developmental psychologist Howard Gardener described nine types of intelligence. He explained that humans have different types of intelligence, although only a few of them are ever tested and discovered at school. You can be smart in nature, music, math, language, understanding, life, interpersonal relationships, physical ability, intelligence, and space. In other words, there is a lot more genius in you than you realize. You will never know what you are capable of until you set big, audacious goals and utilize your talents to achieve them.

What's your dream? To own a couple of rental properties? To have a million in savings? To write a book? To have a successful blog? Well behaved people rarely make history. Only people who attempt the unreasonable achieve the impossible. Why not own 1,000 rentals? Earn a million a month? Write a book every year? Have a successful television program?

ZERO THINKING!

The only difference between someone who earns $10,000, $100,000 or $1,000,000 is their thinking. Each person has the same amount of time. But with each zero comes a new type of thinking. In fact, the person who earns the most works far less than the person who earns the least. The difference in zeros is between your ears!

Change your thinking, and you'll change your life.

Nelson Mandela was the world's most famous prisoner. He had been painted as a dangerous revolutionary, yet his moral authority had never been compromised after spending twenty-seven years behind bars. He was about to be released to a crowd of 50,000.

"As I walked out the door toward the gate that would lead to my freedom," said Mandela, "I knew if I didn't leave my bitterness and hatred behind, I'd still be in prison."

Move your mind to move your life.

THINK SMARTER

Mikimoto Kōkichi was the Japanese entrepreneur who created the first cultured pearl. He put a grain of sand inside a shell and subsequently starting the cultured pearl industry. The Mikimoto business went on to open stores in Paris, New York, Chicago, Los Angeles, Bombay, and Shanghai. Mikimoto was the official jeweler of the Miss USA and Miss Universe pageants. In 2011 the company's estimated total sales were $300 million.

Do you want to be the person who shucks thousands of oyster shells to earn a wage or the person who creates a pearl empire?

Think bigger and think smarter.

THINK FASTER.

The secret to achieving dreams faster is to write them more often.

Pick ten dreams you have for the year and write them every morning. Writing them daily tunes your mind to action. If you're writing a weight loss goal every morning it keeps you fixed on the goal to eat healthily for the day, rather than revisiting your dream list a month later, only to be reminded you should have been eating better. Put a notepad by your bed. Writing goals on a daily basis helps focus you to achieve them faster.

Never be average. What if you took massive action? With massive action comes problems. Awesome! Problems are opportunities that bring results. If you want massive results, then take massive action! What if you packed in your job today to pursue your dream?

A group of American men were surveyed about their biggest fear. They said it was losing their job. The same men were interviewed several years later. They said that losing their job was the best thing that had happened to them because now they were doing something better. I'm not saying be reckless. I'm advocating bigger thinking, which goes hand-in-hand with calculated risk taking.

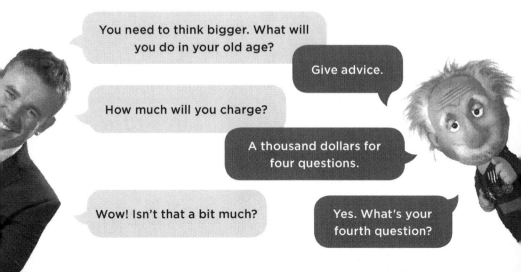

THINK DIFFERENT

Your belief system directly impacts your thought life and therefore your actions. If you want to shift your mindset, then you need to shift your beliefs.

What's the one thing in life that, if you did it, would guarantee you better results?

Why aren't you doing it?

Because you hold a belief that needs shifting. For instance, you may think that making cold sales calls will get you the results you want. Why aren't you making the calls then? Because you believe you will be rejected if you do. Now let's shift your mindset to believing that you have a great *product* and people will *love* to buy from you. You are suddenly freshly motivated to pick up the phone. Your belief system shifted and it produced new results.

What mindset are you falsely believing?

My daughter was upset. My wife consoled her, only to realize she held a false belief over what had happened. After having the truth explained to her, my daughter softened and bounced happily out the room. She didn't need consoling. She needed a mind shift, which produced a positive action.

If you want to think bigger, you need to shift an old belief system. What do you believe that is false? What belief do you need to change to get a bigger result?

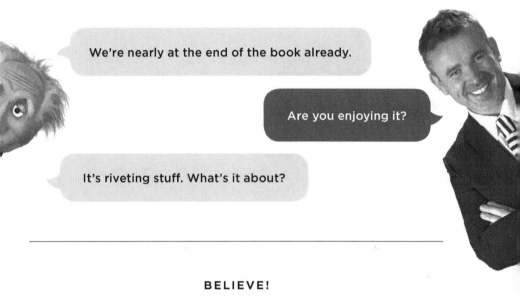

We're nearly at the end of the book already.

Are you enjoying it?

It's riveting stuff. What's it about?

BELIEVE!

Tara Holland believed. Her dream, as a little girl, was to win the Miss America pageant. Despite not achieving success in multiple pageants, she continued to believe in her dream. After failing in one particular pageant, she locked herself away in her hotel room and rented hundreds of beauty pageant videos, which she went on to watch repeatedly.

After winning Miss America in 1997, Tara was asked if she had been nervous. "Not at all," she replied, "I'd won a thousand times before!"

She had pictured and repeatedly imagined herself winning.

You have to see your dream before it can happen, which brings this book full circle. Let's end the book by starting your dream list. Start by writing a list of 100 dreams. The first twenty are easy to dream up. After that you'll need to start digging a little deeper.

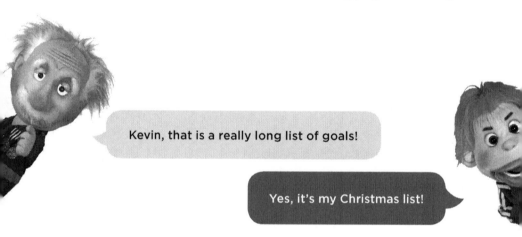

You can think big or you can think small.

What do you *really* want?

MY 100 DREAMS

1. _____

2. _____

3. _____

4. _____

5. _____

6. _____

7. *Subscribe to Marc's YouTube and Twitter.*

8. _____

9. _____

10. _____

11. _____

12. _____

13. _____

14. _____

15. _____

16. _____

17. _____

18. _____

19. _____

20. _____

We're supposed to be writing our dreams. What are you doing?

A puzzle to improve my IQ Can you help me?

What's it supposed to be?

A tiger!

Put the Frosted Flakes back in their box!

21. _____

22. _____

23. _____

24. _____

25. _____

26. _____

27. _____

28. _____

29. _____

30. _____

31. _____

32. _____

33. _____

34. _____

35. _____

36. _____

37. _____

38. _____

39. _____

40. _____

41. _____

42. _____

43. _____

44. _____

45. _____

46. _____

47. _____

48. _____

49. _____

50. _____

51. _____

52. _____

53. _Order Marc's other book._____

54. _____

55. _____

56. _____

57. _____

58. _____

59. _____

60. _____

61. _____

62. _____

63. _____

64. _____

65. _____

66. _____

67. _____

68. _____

69. _____

70. _____

71. _____

72. _____

73. _____

74. _____

75. _____

76. _____

77. _____

78. _____

79. _____

80. _____

81. _____

82. _____

83. _____

84. _____

85. _____

86. _____

87. _____

88. _____

89. _____

90. _____

91. _____

92. _____

93. _____

94. _____

95. _____

96. _____

97. _____

98. _____

99. _____

100. _____

Us seniors are really good dreamers!

Especially when sitting in a recliner after a big meal!

"Don't look back. You're not going that way."

SUMMARY

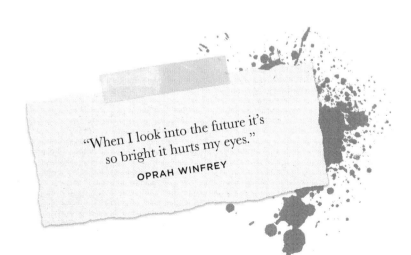

"When I look into the future it's so bright it hurts my eyes."

OPRAH WINFREY

Thanks for reading my book. Your time is precious, which is why I cut out the waffle. A lot of self-help books take an idea, put a new take on it, and then pad it out into a book that you have to wade through trying to find the gold.

How do you read a self-help book? I highlight anything that jumps out at me. When I've finished the book I re-read all the highlighted parts and re-write the best of those on the back page. I know I won't read the book again, but I can now flip open the back cover and re-read the main points to get pumped up. I maximize my book so I can read more!

I also transcribe any gold I find into my life journal, which is packed with dreams and inspiration. Whenever a giant or disappointment tries to get me down, my journal gives me an instant pick-up.

Did he say to write in the book? Shameless!

I never write in books. I draw pictures.

Pictures are fine, too!

What's black and white and read all over?

Not this book!

THE BEST BITS!

To save you strumming through the pages again, here is what you learned:

- You were born a winner and you still are.
- Today is a new beginning.
- Happiness is free, but dreams are not.
- People with dreams move forwards. People without dreams go backwards.
- You're going to live a life of no regrets by not getting stuck at Half Way House.
- Every new goal you set gives you purpose.
- You define what success is for you by the goals you set.
- You know what you really want when you are able to clearly write your goals.

- You either go for your dreams or end up serving someone else's.

- It's up to you. You're not playing the "blame game" anymore.

- Stop talking and start doing.

- You're going to put on your boots and kick the ball.

- You're going to put your ladder on a firm foundation and start climbing.

- You're going to keep stepping!

- Self-discipline is the variable that separates champions from the crowd.

- Regret is worse than fear. Don't live with regret.

- You can take a small step or you can take a big step. Just step!

- Giants are gateways to promotion.

- You are appointed to succeed.

- It's not if you fall, it's how quick you get back up again.

- Fuel-up with daily encouragement and motivation.

- Maximize your time. Now is what you have, and now is when you start.

- You can think big or you can think small.

- Writing your dreams daily makes you achieve them faster.

Dreaming is ultimately all about going from A to B and having the self-discipline to walk out the steps.

I also gave you a lot of keys, practical wisdom, and inspirational quotes to copy and paste on your car, fridge, and journal.

THREE BIG MOMENTS!

There are three key moments in accomplishing your dreams:

The day you write them.
The day you take responsibility for them.
The day you take action.

It's then just a matter of time and discipline until they come to reality.

So were you looking for an easy fix? A massive revelation on how to be happy? I hope this book has helped you think more clearly, but ultimately finding true happiness is all about the choices you make. Although dreaming and progression is an integral part of your overall happiness, never make the mistake

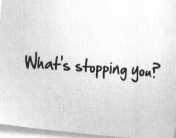

What's stopping you?

of attaching your worth to the achievement of dreams or to thinking you are better or worse than others by whether you do or don't succeed.

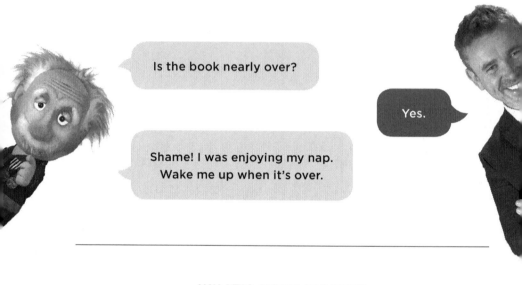

WHAT'S YOUR WORTH?

Sometimes, when speaking to teenagers, I use the illustration of the $20 bill. I ask them how much the crisp, pristine bill in my hand is worth and if anyone wants it. All hands go up. I scrunch it up and ask them again. All hands go up. I tell them drug dealers have used it, it was washed down a toilet and dropped in a cow pat. How much is it worth now? Still $20! Who wants it? All hands go up. The $20 value remains the same, regardless of what it's been through. So does yours. Your value remains the same and is independent of what you choose to do.

Happiness is a choice. Happiness is free. Happiness is always in the now. But goals and dreams have a cost. They are in your future and whether you do or don't accomplish them comes down to the choices you make in the now.

Will your story have a happy ending? I hope so, but ultimately that's up to you.

Carpe diem! Seize the day. Make your life extraordinary!

It's been a pleasure to spend time with you. I hope we get to spend more time together on Twitter, YouTube, in my next book, or at a live event. Until then, to show my appreciation, I enclose a free gift to help you on the next step of your exciting journey.

OTHER BOOKS
BY MARC GRIFFITHS

DREAM STEALER This fast-paced action novel (for ages 10+) follows Kevin, who is placed in Greystones, a scary school for unwanted children. Kevin escapes the clutches of Mr. East, the one-eyed beast, only to be caught by Lawrence Pudding-Pig, a bully who is even nastier than his name sounds, and locked in the Forbidden Turret, where he discovers a secret. Together, with his friend Misty, they venture through worlds of dice, dwarfs, talking animals and the impossible to discover the power of dreams. Dare you read it? We take no responsibility for what may happen to you…but always be aware of the Dream Stealer!

BE HAPPY!: IT'S *NOT* A SECRET, I KNOW HOW!
Q: What's the best thing you can do for you?
A: BE HAPPY!
Why? Because when you're happy, everyone in your sphere of influence benefits. Most people are so busy trying to get happy and find meaning that they never *are* happy! Inspirational ventriloquist, Marc Griffiths, and his puppet team hilariously unpack the five essential areas of life in which you need to BE HAPPY!

Speedy
the Sloth

I hope I wake up in time to make
it into the next book!

ABOUT THE AUTHOR

MARC GRIFFITHS has addressed more than a million people in over 5,000 talks.

As a keynote speaker he has researched, written, and spoken for twenty-five years, speaking to all types of audiences on the subjects of Happiness, Personal and Professional Development, Self-Esteem, Goals, and Dream achievement.

His humor and ventriloquism make his talks exciting and different, while his inspiration and wisdom bring immediate and long-term results.

Originally from the UK, Marc speaks internationally but now lives in Atlanta with his wife and four children.

He said all that without moving his mouth!

GET HAPPY!
In 57 $\frac{1}{2}$ seconds

THE FUN WEEKLY VIDEO BLOG ON You Tube

Subscribe!

GETOUTYOURBOX1

WEBSITE

www.getoutyourbox.com

YOUTUBE

getoutyourbox1

TWITTER

mventriloquist

FACEBOOK

Inspirational Ventriloquist

Come on! Push the follow button!
I know what I'm doing. I'll be setting
up chitchat on Snappitychat soon!

87786294R00133

Made in the USA
Columbia, SC
27 January 2018